Kenzaburo Oë

Kenzaburo Oë was born in 1935, in Ose village in Shikoku, Western Japan. He has won every major national prize, many international awards, including the 1989 Prix Europalia, and the Nobel Prize for Literature in 1994. His novels include *Scream, The Perverts, Adventures in Daily Life, Hiroshima Notebooks* and *A Personal Matter.*

Also by Kenzaburo Oë in Picador

A Personal Matter

Nip the Buds Shoot the Kids

Kenzaburo Oë

TRANSLATED AND INTRODUCED BY

Paul St John Mackintosh and Maki Sugiyama

PICADOR

First published Great Britain 1995 by Marion Boyars Publishers

This edition published 1996 by Picador
an imprint of Macmillan Publishers Ltd
25 Eccleston Place, London SW1W 9NF
and Basingstoke

Associated companies throughout the world

ISBN 0 330 34729 2

1 3 5 7 9 8 6 4 2

A CIP catalogue record for this book is available
from the British Library

Printed and bound in Great Britain

Introduction

'That Man should Labour & sorrow, & learn & forget, & return
To the dark valley whence he came, to begin his labour anew'
— William Blake, *Vala, or the Four Zoas*, Night the Eighth

Memushiri kouchi (*Nip the Buds, Shoot the Kids*, 1958) was an assured novelistic debut by a young student who had already become a national literary figure. Kenzaburo Oe was fortunate in that much of his fictional domain was presented to him as a child. He was born in 1935, the third son of a large family, in the village of Ose in Ehime Prefecture, nestled in a valley deep in the mountainous interior of Shikoku, itself one of the more isolated and peripheral of Japan's main islands. His family were near the apex of village society, their status symbolized by the family storehouse, with its traditional earth floor, and by his father's official monopoly of the bark-stripping business which provided raw material for banknote paper. His grandmother brought him up on the folk tales and traditions of his unusual native place. Other 20th-century Japanese writers have been raised in equally remote places — Kenji Miyazawa in rural Iwate Prefecture, Osamu Dazai in the distant Tsugaru Peninsula, Kobo Abe in Manchuria — but Oe seems to have felt uniquely elected from the start as a man of the periphery, the margins, and as the custodian of his marginal community's heritage.

The studious, introverted boy grew up in the unreal atmosphere of wartime Japan. In his novel *Okurete kita seinen (The Youth Who Came Late,* 1962), he describes the patriotic ritual that typical schoolchildren of the time endured. Each pupil was asked by the teacher, 'What would you do if the emperor asked you to die?'; each would answer 'I would cut open my belly and die, sir'. The story's narrator was tormented by the knowledge that his response was a lie. Oe himself dreamed of this terrifying god, the Emperor, as a great white bird swooping on him out of the sky. On another occasion, he recalled, a dog killer came to requisition the pelts of all the village dogs for military use. With commendable obedience, the villagers brought out all their animals. The dog killer poleaxed and skinned them and took the pelts away, but the skins were later found abandoned outside the village. Oe regarded this as his first experience of the meaninglessness of violence. His father died during the war; then a further disturbance came with the defeat of Japan, when the Emperor, the living god, spoke on the radio for the first time in the voice of an ordinary man to announce the surrender. Soon after, the first Americans appeared, dispensing candy instead of incendiary bombs. The values of Oe's upbringing were inverted: the most fanatical militarist of his teachers became the most fervent democrat, and his education was finished under the new democratizing regime imposed by the Occupation authorities, a regime whose own values were compromised by the 'Red Purge' of Communists conducted by the American occupation authorities at the start of the Korean War. Oe's view from the edge of his own culture, and his nostalgia for the elemental simplicities of his childhood, became interwoven with a powerful critical insight.

Oe's first love was mathematics, but his interests soon shifted. 'I was a mathematical boy until then. I lost interest in mathematics and started reading literature...[at my first year in Junior High] I learned the Junior High School textbook and the Senior High's, then there was nothing left to do.' This early scientific bent prefigured the extremely, deliberately intellectual nature of his approach, a contrast to the supposedly anti-rational, 'spontaneous' mainstream of Japanese letters. When he went up to the elite Tokyo University in 1954, it was to study French literature. In conversation with Kazuo Ishiguro, he recalled how 'around that time my grandmother died, and my mother was getting older. The legends and traditions and folklore of my village were being lost. Meanwhile, here I was in Tokyo, imagining and trying to remember those things. The act of trying to remember and the act of creating began to overlap. And that is the reason why I began to write novels. I tried to write them using the methods of French literature that I had studied.' His first stories began to appear in student magazines and other periodicals, and in 1958 his story *Shiiku (Prize Stock)* won the Akutagawa Prize, Japan's foremost literary award for new writers. Set in an unnamed village in wartime, it presented the community's custody of a black American airman in an almost mythical light. *Memushiri kouchi (Nip the Buds, Shoot the Kids)* also appeared that year. Oe was only 23 years old.

Unlike *Prize Stock* (one of the stories collected in *Teach Us to Outgrow Our Madness*), which integrated the boy narrator with his community, *Nip the Buds* presents its hero as an absolute outsider, a delinquent ostracized by the unbelievably brutish and callous villagers. Oe's anger against his elders' sheeplike complicity in the disastrous militarist adventure, against the generals who led the people to the end of the road only to abandon them, against the craven reversal of ideologies, is venomously evident. He has stressed how the novel was rooted in his wartime experiences. 'It had only been thirteen years since the war. The war was deeply tied to my life as if it had ended yesterday. All I had to do was let my war experiences, not factual but mental, take their own course and write them down.' But the nameless village is as symbolic as Camus' Oran, Melville's *Pequod* or Golding's desert island. The book, which has only a handful of proper names in it and virtually no identifiable reference in it to any actual time or place, occupies a generalized realm of the mythic imagination. The brother-motif at the centre of the plot has a multiple significance typical of this mythic dimension. 'I placed at the pivot of the structure a young boy as "the older brother" and an infant as "the younger brother". This "younger brother" was often the being that manifested "hermaphroditism" for "the older brother".' The hermaphrodite enjoys a primordial power as the transcender of differences, the meeting point of the universe's opposing forces, and this cosmic significance is grafted by Oe onto his narrator through the device of brotherhood, indicating that his ambitions in the novel go well beyond the critical or satirical.

The narrative of *Nip the Buds* hinges on the delinquents' creation of their own autonomous time, outside history, replete with the elemental richness of 'primitive' being. 'Time won't move a step without grown-ups' orders.' (Oe has consistently returned to this theme, with greater sophistication since his encounter with the ideas of Mircea Eliade.) The drama is ontological as much as political: the forest surrounding the village is a seething chaos lapping at the perimeter of the human order; the boys' idyll of freedom is ended not by the cruel villagers but by the tragic resurgence of death, which snatches away the narrator's lover and his brother. Betrayed even by his comrades and bereft of all human accommodation, the boy finally runs blindly off into the dark void. Oe later became an enthusiastic reader of William Blake, citing in particular the quotation from *Vala, or the Four Zoas* which heads this introduction as a key to his enthusiasm for the Cockney visionary. The overtones of Eros and Thanatos, Alpha and Omega in that couplet are as essential to Oe as its spirit of *re-enracinement* that he later espoused.

Critical reaction to the novel was generally enthusiastic, though its style prefigured a contentious aspect of Oe's writing. Oe has retained an interest in both Western poets such as Blake and Yeats and Eastern lyricists like Kenji Miyazawa and the Korean poet Kim Chi Ha. His complex, impacted style, often redolent of Sartre's quasi-

Heideggerean density, has a consistent poetic ambition. There was also an ideological slant to his quarrel with the supposed 'vagueness' of Japanese, a slant couched in grotesque, earthy imagery and a clotted, overly specified syntax resembling English. His usual working method is first to write a straightforward Japanese sentence, then go over it two or three times, each time bending it out of its usual shape and making it more refractory, highly worked and polysemic. Nothing could be further from the traditional limpidity of Japanese style exemplified by a writer like Shiga Naoya, whose mellifluous clarity obscures a desperately suspect literary ideology of 'sincerity' and 'purity of spirit' espoused by many Japanese, especially of the pre-war generations.

This same ideology, which centres on what writer and readers agree on in advance as the genuine sentiments of the heart, is strongly opposed to the novel of ideas, and Oe's use of highly developed ideas to structure his works further exacerbates his quarrel with Japanese literary traditionalism. Added to this is an espousal of the writer's public role far removed from traditional aestheticism. Drawing on Claude Levi-Strauss, Oe has declared that 'the role of literature . . . is to create a model of a contemporary age which envelops past and future and a human model that lives in that age.' In the Japanese context, he took this duty for his generation of writers to be the articulation of new principles to guide the nation, after the débâcle of 1945 exploded the authoritarian ideology which had governed Japan since the Meiji Restoration of 1868.

Oe later revisited *Nip the Buds* in *'Memushiri kouchi' saiban* (*The Trial of 'Nip the Buds, Shoot the Kids'*, 1980), which comments on the original work in a fashion that dramatizes the evolution of his style. Employing a slew of post-modern techniques (for Oe is never less than a fully self-conscious writer), he presents a fictional 'author', outcast because of a novel which accused his native village. This writer learns from his younger brother of another, older brother, the hero of *Nip the Buds*, who returns to the village after the war in the company of American troops and in the guise of his younger brother (drowned in a flood), to put the community on trial. Proceedings in the closed hearing are conveyed to the villagers through a re-enactment which becomes a ritual festival involving the whole community. In the end, the accuser's case fails and he leaves for America, fighting in Vietnam, where he is crippled. This vastly increased complexity is typical of Oe's later practice

Oe left Tokyo University in 1959 with a graduation thesis on Sartre, married (1960) Yukari, the sister of film director Juzo (*Tampopo*) Itami, a friend from his high school days in Shikoku, and settled down to life as a full-time writer. He wrote of Japan's post-war situation, its ambivalent relationship with its conquerors/liberators and the anomie of the young intellectual, thus losing some of the broader resonance of *Nip the Buds*. The outsiders of this period tended to establish their autonomous domains as subway perverts or sex murderers. His two serial stories of 1961, *Sebunteen (Seventeen)* and *Seiji shonen shishu (Death of a Political Youth)* were based on the assassination in 1960 of the Socialist Party leader, Inejiro Asanuma, by a seventeen-year-old right-winger, Otoya Yamaguchi, who subsequently committed suicide in prison. This was the era of mass left-wing demonstrations against the re-negotiation of Japan's security treaty (Ampo) with the United States and the high water mark of post-war political tension. The so-called Ampo demonstrations filled Tokyo's streets with hundreds of thousands of radicals, and revolution seemed a constant possibility. In this heated climate, right-wing extremists bitterly attacked the stories and their author, and the magazine issued a humble apology for any offence caused and withdrew the second story from circulation. To this day it can only be found in a few library collections. Leftist radicals then castigated Oe's cowardice. Oe himself protested that both sides had misunderstood his position, which 'never, at any point, treated the hero with ridicule'. He later ascribed such occurrences to the perpetuation of the 'emperor system', which he felt had remained a focus for the worst impulses in the Japanese nation, as dramatized by Yukio Mishima's histrionic, camped-up suicide. 'The curse of the emperor system', and the valorization of all such centres of power at the expense of peripheral loci like Okinawa, has remained the butt of his fierce criticism.

Oe's concerns were redirected soon after by tragic events which catalyzed his development from a major writer into a great one. In October 1962 an old friend, an economist married to a Frenchwoman and living in Paris, hanged himself during the Cuban Missile Crisis, leaving behind a suicide note telling of his terror in the face of the impending nuclear holocaust. Then in 1963 his first son was born with a cerebral hernia, a lesion of the skull through which brain tissue protruded in a grotesque red growth. Oe's agonized struggle over what to do is chronicled in his novel *Kojinteki na taiken (A Personal Matter,* 1964). As if in defiance of the darkness waiting to swallow the child, he named it Hikari (Light). His tortured feelings were exemplified by his actions when he visited Hiroshima that summer to attend a conference on global nuclear disarmament. Bon, the Japanese festival of All Souls, ends when the dead are sent back to their rest in lantern boats inscribed with their names, launched onto the waters at night. Similar services have been instituted at Hiroshima and Nagasaki on the anniversaries of the bombings, to rest the victims' souls. Oe went along with a friend whose daughter had just died, and when that friend wrote his daughter's name on a lantern, Oe wrote Hikari's, realizing afterwards that he was treating his son as one of the dead. Much later, he recalled that he had added his own name. On returning to Tokyo, he agreed to surgery which closed the lesion in Hikari's skull, at the cost of permanent brain damage.

Oe's visit to Hiroshima was decisive in more ways than one. He met with and interviewed a number of survivors of the Hiroshima bomb, later publishing the interviews and his impressions as *Hiroshima noto* (*Hiroshima Notes*, 1964). All these influences pooled in Oe's imagination to produce the remarkable fusion of private and public concerns, ontological and historical consciousness, in his 1967 masterpiece *Man'en gannen no futtoboru* (translated as *The Silent Cry*), which opens with the birth of a deformed child and the death of a man who hangs himself with his head painted red and a cucumber thrust up his anus, and closes with the narrator's redemption. The book was being serialized when Oe discovered the religious thought of the Romanian scholar-poet Mircea Eliade, with its emphasis on the annihilation/purification of history through ritual repetition, prompting him to withdraw the draft and reshape it into a work which became a watershed in his career as well as probably the greatest postwar Japanese novel.

The Silent Cry presents yet another pair of brothers,

returning to their native village: a village whose mythical founder fled there in fear of the terrible monster, the 'Chosokabe', which fills all time and space. 'Chosokabe' was in fact the name of the clan which dominated Oe's area of Shikoku in the sixteenth century, and this 'monster' is therefore history, from which the villagers fled to establish their own autonomous time. But the narrator returns to his origins to confront history, a century of family history which echoes backwards and forwards across the generations. His brother Takashi, a charismatic, psychopathic radical and a frightful distillation of the terrorist personality, has his own violent methods for creating a dialogue with history. The novel embraces both general themes and the minute details of contemporary life: only Oe could find universal significance in the proliferation of supermarkets and closure of village shops in the early Sixties. He developed this approach to tackle what he saw as Japan's modern deracination and cultural plight. 'I can think of no people or nation as much in need of a clue for self-recovery as the Japanese . . . whose culture evidences a strange blending of first and third world cultures'.

In *Dojidai gemu (Contemporary Games,* 1979) Oe once more returns to his native domain to redeem it from history, emphasizing its marginality and dramatizing its imagined war against the Greater Empire of Japan. He also treats the small community's crimes more indulgently than those of the larger body it opposes. Oe retells virtually the same story in *M/T to mori no fushigi no monogatari (M/T and the Marvels of the Forest,* 1986), repeating a familiar pattern in his voluminous oeuvre whereby the possibilities of a single situation are fully exhausted through repetition and variation. This tallies with the choice-centred cosmology Oe put into the mouth of one of his characters in *A Personal Matter*: 'Every time you stand at a crossroads of life and death, you have two universes in front of you . . . various universes emerge around each of us'. Oe's later tales sometimes lose this existential urgency by making the community their hero, in keeping with his later desire to recover a rooted identity. They often recall magic realism, which he has explored through his own version of Bakhtin's Rabelaisian 'grotesque realism': a fertile discipline for the mature Oe that even accommodates the conventions of genre fiction, as in the bestselling science-fiction novel *Chiryo to (The Treatment Tower*, 1990), which also digs deeply into his environmental concerns.

Oe has also acknowledged the usefulness of structuralism for him, thus becoming one of the first great writers to benefit from both the first and second waves of French post-Heideggerian thought: 'Speaking for myself, as one writer, I evaluate very highly the diversified cultural thoughts springing forth from structuralism, for they provide a strong and vital incentive in the field of literature.' He has been characterized as 'the eloquent modernist spokesman who has consistently resisted aspects of postmodernist theories as they have travelled to Japan', but this relates more to the uncritical absorption of fashionable foreign theories by an increasingly sterile Japanese intelligensia. Despite his easy communion with worldwide intellectual culture, Oe himself has expressed doubts about the value of his work to non-Japanese readers: 'I write my books for Japanese readers, rather than for foreign. Moreover, the Japanese readers I have in mind are a limited group. The people I wrote for are people of my own generation, people who have had the same experiences as myself.'

This somewhat pessimistic evaluation is contradicted by the high esteem Oe enjoys internationally and the numerous translations published. His global stature, recognized by the award of the Prix Europalia in 1990, was consecrated by the 1994 Nobel Prize for Literature. The Nobel citation described Kenzaburo Oe as a writer who 'with poetic force creates an imagined world where life and myth condense to form a disconcerting picture of the human predicament today.'

Japanese television broadcasts were interrupted by special bulletins announcing the news. With characteristic modesty, Oe attributed his success to 'the accomplishments of modern Japanese literature', paying particular tribute to his predecessors Kobo Abe and Masuji Ibuse. In an equally characteristic gesture, he declined the Imperial Order of Culture customarily given to Japanese Nobel Prize-winners, provoking angry protests from a handful of right-wingers who took this as an insult to the throne. The general public response was enthusiastic, though somewhat bemused by the work itself, and the news prompted some reflection on Japan's position in world culture. Oe has often demanded that Japan should re-examine its past and its culture to find a future beyond its present 'grotesquely bloated consumer society'. It would be ironic if it was the triumph of this writer, weaned on cultures far removed from that of Japan, which provoked just such a re-examination.

In his Nobel lecture entitled 'Japan, the Ambiguous, and Myself', which he delivered in English, Oe further enlarged on Japan's present plight, riven by an 'ambiguity so powerful and penetrating that it splits both the state and its people'. The ambiguous condition of his country, 'ori-

entated toward learning from and imitating the West'
since the onset of its modernization, yet an East Asian
nation which 'has firmly maintained its traditional culture', is for Oe 'a kind of chronic disease that has been
prevalent throughout the modern age.' He outlined his
personal strategy for tackling the issue: 'the fundamental
style of my writing has been to start from my personal
matters and then to link it up with society, the state and the
world.' He touched on the matter of his son Hikari, who
as a baby 'responded only to the chirps of wild birds and
never to human voices,' yet 'was awakened by the voices of
birds to the music of Bach and Mozart'. And he affirmed
his faith in the 'exquisite healing power of art', which
might 'enable both those who express themselves with
words and their readers to recover from their own sufferings
and the sufferings of their time'. The possible result of a
final resolution of ambiguity, 'a desirable Japanese identity', Oe defined with George Orwell's term 'decent', 'a
synonym of "humanist" '.

Paradoxically, having finished his latest work, the trilogy
Moeageru midori no ki (The Blazing Green Tree, 1993-5) Oe
declared that he would abandon fiction. For Hikari, who
lives in Tokyo with his parents, had triumphed despite his
severe handicap through his native musical ability, com-
posing delightful and moving music which enjoys healthy
sales. A recent NHK documentary, filmed a few months
before the Nobel Prize award on the occasion of a concert
of Hikari's music at a school for the handicapped in
Hiroshima, showed father and son together as artists. With
Hikari now able to express himself, Oe declared that he no
longer felt obligated to speak for him, and that all his
fiction had not let him understand the son who could

compose such music. He left open the possibility of trying essays or new forms of writing.

Looking back much later on *Nip the Buds*, Oe said of it: 'I think that this novel was the happiest work for me. I could openly release my childhood memories, both the bitter and the sweet ones, into the imagery of the novel. It was even a pleasure. Now I no longer feel that liberation which accompanied the pleasure of writing.'

NIP THE BUDS SHOOT THE KIDS

Chapter One:

Arrival

Two of our boys had escaped during the night, so at dawn we still hadn't left. We spent a while hanging out our stiff green coats, wet from the night before, in the pale sunshine and watched the umber river beyond the fig trees on the far side of the footpath behind the low hedge. Yesterday's violent rain had cracked the path, and clear water was flowing in those sharply etched cracks. Swollen by rain and melted snow and water from the breached reservoir, the ferociously roaring river was bearing away at tremendous speed the corpses of dogs, cats and rats.

Then the village women and children came running out along the path to gaze at us with eyes full of curiosity, timidity and dull insolence, exchanging low feverish whispers and abrupt bursts of laughter, which annoyed us. To them, we were complete aliens. Some of us went up to the hedge, flaunting immature penises like reddish apricots at the villagers. Elbowing her way through the children's giggling agitation, a middle-aged woman pressed forward to stare with tightly pursed lips and laughed red-faced as she relayed lewd details to her friends carrying babies. But this game had been repeated many times in various other villages, and we no longer enjoyed the excitable peasant women's shameless overreaction to our genitals, circumcised in the usual way for reformatory boys.

We decided to ignore the villagers standing obdurately behind the hedge and staring at us. Some of us walked around on our side of the hedge like beasts in a cage; others sat on sun-dried stepping stones and gazed at the faint leaf-shadows on the dark brown earth, tracing their trembling bluish outlines with their fingertips.

Only my brother stared back at the villagers, leaning on the hedge and wetting the front of his coat on the hard, leathery camellia leaves dappled with water droplets from the fog. For my brother, the villagers were bizarre creatures who awakened his curiosity. From time to time he would run up to me and chatter in my ear in a shrill excited voice, enthusiastically describing the children's trachomatous eyes and chapped lips, and the women's huge fingers, blackened and broken from farm work. Under the villagers' scrutiny, I took pride in my brother's glowing rosy cheeks and the beauty of his liquid irises.

Nonetheless, for aliens like captured wild beasts to be safe before others watching them, it is best to lead the will-less, eyeless existence of a stone, flower or tree: a purely observed existence. My brother, since he persisted in being the eye that watched the villagers, was struck on his cheeks by thick yellowish gobs of spittle rolled on the women's tongues, and stones thrown by the children. But, smiling, he would wipe his cheeks with his large bird-embroidered pocket facecloth and go on staring in wonderment at the villagers who had insulted him.

That meant that my brother had not yet grown used to this observed existence, the status of a caged beast. But the rest of us were certainly used to it. We had really grown used to a lot of things. We could only beat our way forward, forced to twist bodies and minds to mould ourselves to the many things that confronted us daily, one after another. Being beaten, bleeding and keeling over was only the beginning, and our comrades who for a month had been detailed to look after police dogs carved obscenities on walls and floorboards with young fingers that had been deformed by bites from the hungry dogs' strong jaws when they fed them each morning. But we really couldn't help feeling unnerved when, later on, our two fugitives came back, following behind the patrolman and the warden. They were so completely done in.

While the warden and the patrolman talked, we stood round our two brave comrades who had failed so miserably. They were black-eyed, with dried blood sticking to their cut lips and their hair matted with blood. I took the alcohol out of my kit-bag, washed their wounds, and daubed them with iodine. One of them, the well-built older boy, had a bruise on his inner thigh from a kick, but when he rolled up his trouser leg we hadn't the faintest idea how to treat it.

'I was going to get away to the port through the wood during the night. I was going to board a ship and go south,' he said ruefully. We laughed raucously, though we were still all on edge. He was always longing for the south and always talking like that, so we called him 'Minami' [South].

'But some peasants found me, so I got a proper beating. I hadn't pinched a single potato. They treat us like rats.'

We gasped in admiration and anger at their courage and the peasants' brutality.

'Hey, we almost got to the road leading to the port, didn't we? Just jump on a freight truck and stow away, then on to the port.'

'Ah,' said the younger boy weakly, 'just a little further.'

'It was all a waste,' said Minami, licking his lips, 'because you got a belly-ache.'

'Yeah,' said the boy, still wan and suffering from persistent stomach-ache, his head bowed in shame.

'The peasants beat you?' said my brother, eyes shining.

'Eh? No way was it like a beating,' Minami said, with a mixture of pride and scorn. 'I got fagged out dodging them, and they were foaming at the mouth, wanting to hammer my backside with their field hoes.'

'Ah,' my brother said in a kind of dreamy rapture, 'hoes on your bum?'

When the patrolman had left after shooing away the throng on the other side of the hedge, the warden called us together. First he struck Minami and his accomplice on their split lips, smearing their chins with fresh blood, then sentenced them to a one-day fast. That was a lenient sentence, and since the way he hit them was not like a warden, or was more like what we regarded as a fine manly trait, we treated him as part of our group's restored integrity.

'All of you, don't try to escape again,' the warden said, opening his youthful throat and blushing. 'In this kind of isolated village, whenever you try to escape, the peasants will catch you before you reach a town. They loathe you like leprosy. They'll kill you without hesitation. You'll find it harder to escape here than from jail.'

That was right. Through our experience of escape and failure as we shifted from village to village, we had learned that we were surrounded by gigantic walls. In the farming villages, we were like splinters stuck in skin. In an instant we would be pressed in on from all sides by coagulating flesh, extruded and suffocated. These farmers, wearing the hard armour of their clannishness, refused to allow others to pass through, let alone settle in. It was we, a small group, who were just drifting on a sea which never took in people from outside but threw them back.

'I'd say we've found the best way to confine you; war's useful sometimes,' said the warden, baring his strong teeth. 'I couldn't hit Minami hard enough to break his front teeth: there must be some peasants with really splendid fists.'

'I was hit with a hoe,' Minami said happily, 'by a flabby old gaffer.'

'Don't speak without permission,' the warden shouted. 'Get ready to leave in five minutes. I aim to reach our destination by evening. If you hang around you won't eat, so hurry!'

Cheering, we broke up and dashed to the old silkworm-rearing shed where we had been assigned our one-day billets to collect our belongings. Five minutes later, when we were ready to depart, Minami's accomplice in the abortive escape attempt was, with little groans, vomiting pale pink filth in the corner of the hedge. We stood in line on the footpath and sang our slow, effeminate, lascivious and shocking reformatory song, belting out the long refrain crammed with religious symbolism, until his spasms had subsided. The astonished villagers surrounded us fifteen undernourished singing boys in our green waterproofs. Our chests heaved with the customary humiliation and black rage.

When the boy got back in line after vomiting, noisily trying to snort up a wheat grain stuck in his nostril, we set out with our canvas shoes pattering, hastily shouting out the third refrain of our song.

It was a time of killing. Like a long deluge, the war sent its mass insanity flooding into the convolutions of people's feelings, into every last recess of their bodies, into the forests, the streets and into the sky. An airman had even frantically strafed the courtyard of the old brick building where we were housed, descending suddenly from the sky, a young blond airman rudely sticking out his bum inside the partially transparent fuselage of his warplane. Early next morning, when we filed out for our detail, a woman who had just died of starvation, and whose body was still leaning just outside the gate's spiteful barbed-wire entanglements, collapsed right in front of our commanding warden's nose. Most of the night, and sometimes in broad daylight, fires from air raids lit up the sky over the town or smeared it with blackish smoke.

In that time, when maddened adults ran riot in the streets, it is enough to record that there was a strange mania for locking up those with skin that was smooth all over, or with just a little glowing chestnut down; those who had committed petty offences; including those simply judged to have criminal tendencies.

With the air raids intensifying, and terminal symptoms beginning to appear, the reformatory inmates' families finally began to take them back, but the majority never came forward to pick up their bad, troublesome offspring. So the wardens, with an obsessive determination to hang on to their spoils, planned a mass evacuation of the boys.

With two weeks still to go before the evacuation, the last letters from families asking to take their children back had been sent, and the inmates were in a fever of anticipation. When, in the first week, my father, who had once reported me, turned up wearing army boots and a war worker's cap, accompanied by my younger brother, I was overcome with joy. However, the truth of the matter was that my father, worn out by searching for a place to evacuate my brother to, had finally hit upon the idea of taking advantage of the reformatory's mass evacuation. I was bitterly disappointed. Even so, after my father had gone home we hugged each other tightly.

My brother, joining us juvenile delinquents and forced to wear the uniform, was beside himself with fascination and joy for the first two or three days. After that, he talked to the others incessantly, eyes wet with veneration, pestering them for intimate details of their misdeeds; and when night fell, lying with me under the same blanket, breathing heavily, he mulled over the atrocious experiences he had just heard about. Then, since he had memorized the others' sparkling, bloody histories, he was wild to invent his own imaginary crimes. From time to time he would come running up to me and, blushing, tell me such fantasies as shooting a girl's eye out with his toy gun. In the end my brother slipped smooth as water into the life of our group. In that time of killing, that time of madness, we children may have been the only ones to develop a close solidarity. Then, with the two weeks of anticipation and disappointment over, our gang, including my brother, set out on our strangely proud and shameful journey.

Departure: that was what made us sally forth from the unbelievably weird and decrepit orange perimeter fence; but it left us no freer. It was as though we were marching along a passageway linking two cellars. The galling orange fence was replaced by countless new wardens with calloused farmers' hands. The degree of freedom we were granted on our journey was no more than what we had enjoyed inside the fence. The only new pleasure we got from going outside the fence was that we could stare and scoff at a great number of 'pure' boys.

Right from the start, whenever we made our repeated, irrepressible escape attempts, we were recaptured by hostile grown-ups in villages, woods, rivers and fields, and brought back more dead than alive. For us, who came from a faraway city, the villages were like a thick transparent rubber wall. If we burrowed into it we would soon be squeezed out.

Consequently, the only freedoms we could enjoy were walking on the village roads which sent up fierce clouds of dust or drowned ankles in mud; or watching for a lapse in the warden's vigilance while we rested in temples, shrines or sheds so that we could do a quick trade with the villagers for some food; or trying to whistle and tempt the village girls as we fretted hopelessly over our travel-stained uniforms.

Our journey should have been over in a week. But because negotiations between our leader and the village headmen designated to accept us had broken down one after another, it was already into the third week. We were supposed to reach the last scheduled location that afternoon: a remote village deep in the mountains. Were it not for the fugitives, we would probably have arrived by now and would be sitting down watching the deliberations of our leader and the village elders or resting stretched out on the ground.

Once the high spirits inspired by the fugitives in our midst had died down, we hurried on in silence, bent forward, our kit-bags pushed back on our hips. Most of us walked deep in thought, sharing a gloom which welled up in our chests and rose into our throats, not to mention the boy groaning with stomach-ache as he walked.

Our journey was almost over. Even if we were just moving in darkness, so long as the journey continued we at least had the chance to try our abortive escapes. But once we went into the vast interior and found a village to settle in beyond the mountain valleys, we would feel shut up in a deep pit, inside thick walls, even more than when we were first put inside the reformatory's orange fence. Then we would be finished. Once the many villages we had journeyed through had closed into a solid ring, I didn't think that we could slip out of it again.

Minami's failure in what was probably the last escape attempt was the main reason for our general discontent. We nursed the same resentment and felt the same anger as Minami towards the boy who had ruined the eagerly-awaited escape attempt with a trivial thing like stomach-ache. When he groaned, we whistled to show our indifference, and some even threw stones at the afflicted boy's backside.

Only my brother comforted him, regardless of our sulky

anger, and questioned Minami about the details of his escape. However, my brother's excitability and good spirits could not dispel the gloom which hung over us all. In the end, once he had grown tired from walking, our group went on, hanging our heads, in our drab, ill-cut clothes, without taking notice of the barking dogs or the farmers and their families who came running out from roadside farmhouses to stare at us. Only the sturdy warden leading us walked with his chest thrust out.

If we had gone on with our half-hearted march, we would never have made it to our destination, even if we had walked until daybreak. But after we had cautiously crossed a dangerous bridge almost washed away by the flood and followed a narrow side road that came out on the broad highway to the next prefecture, we caught sight of wonderfully dignified and ardent uniformed youths: a group of army cadets crowded together and armed middle-aged military policemen standing in the green-striped truck parked next to them. Instantly recovering our spirits, we raised a cheer and went running up to them.

The cadets turned round at our cheers, but they stood stiffly and made no reply. They were armed with short daggers. With their hard faces, half-open mouths and well-shaped heads held straight, they were as beautiful as carefully trained horses. We stopped about a metre away from them and stared at them longingly. No one spoke to them; they too were quiet, looking wan and anxious. These silent cadets, their tender profiles shining in the evening sun peeking through a bare copse on the gentle slope, these young soldiers, silent as if bewildered, exuded an intense, captivating strength like an odour from all over their bodies. It was far stronger than when the cadets dug up and burned pine roots to make thick, gooey and smelly resin or wandering round town with their fine attire and dumb chatter.

'Hey,' Minami said, bringing his head close to mine and almost brushing his lips against my ear, 'If they wanted, I'd sleep with them any time for a handful of hard tack, even if my piles got split and I got all swollen and bunged up.'

He heaved a sigh, saliva collecting at the corners of his pouting lips, and gazed with shining glazed-over eyes at the cadets' strongly rounded, slightly splayed buttocks.

'When I got caught, I was sleeping with someone just like them,' he said, mortification suddenly flooding over his face.

'Eh? You can't call yourself a prostitute over a handful of hard tack,' I said. 'They'll catch a faggot, even if he's not a prostitute.'

'Huh,' he said absent-mindedly and went forward, pushing his mates aside to take a closer look at those who might have been his clients before his imprisonment.

My brother, who was listening eagerly next to the warden and the military policemen as they talked, turned and came running to me, his shoulders quivering with excitement, and spoke to me with the same air of importance as when he whispered secrets.

'He ran away. An army cadet ran away into the forest. Everyone's looking for him. If we go into the forest, we'll be shot.'

'Why?' I asked in astonishment. 'Why did he run away into the forest?'

'He ran away,' he repeated in a frenzy. 'He ran away. He's in the forest.'

When our comrades had gathered round, my brother

repeated the news many times in a sing-song voice. We went up to the military police. The warden ordered us to stand by, waving his arm and pointing to a tree. Then he gave his opinion of the state of the road we had marched along, inviting the MPs to ask him more questions. Gathered at the base of a low camphor tree with spreading branches, growing over-excited, we stamped our feet and grunted in our throats, looking in turn at the cadets sunk in gloom, the MPs pompously questioning the warden, and the brown mountainside growing darker and covered with withered leaves, giving off a purple glow, where the deserter must be hiding. But because of the long time that passed without learning the state of the MPs' deliberations, our ardour cooled and we started to feel discontent.

After the onset of the chill evening air had darkened the MPs' and the warden's features, a man came riding up on an old-fashioned bicycle. He spoke to them, then loaded his bicycle onto the truck. The MPs shouted out loud and the cadets fell in; then the warden came running back to us.

'They said they'll give us a lift to our destination in their truck,' he said.

Instantly we recovered our spirits and scrambled into the truck, yelling. When it set off with a heavy mechanical din we saw, in our excitement, the army cadets starting to file off in the opposite direction.

Wheezing and shuddering violently, the truck went up the steep and narrow night road. In places there were landslides caused by the floods, and then we had to get out of the truck. We waited, watching its dangerous passage, standing ahead of it on the stratified red clay road lit up by its headlamps, narrowing our eyes against the glare. But the middle-aged villager who sat on top of the old-fashioned big-boned bicycle lain flat in the truck as he smoked acrid tobacco made from dried herbs, never tried to get down. He maintained an air of detachment from us and kept quiet, but sometimes he would stare at our skinny shoulders and knees, his horribly bloodshot eyes swivelling painfully. Eventually he turned his gaze away. The truck slowed more and more, the sound of its engine vibrating heedlessly in the thick layers of night air as it ran along the uneven mountain road. Obscure blackish foliage pressed in from both sides of the narrowing road, and a chill, cheek-piercing wind bearing a clammy mist banked down our excitement and kept them smouldering.

Furthermore, the threatening shoulders of the kneeling MP, who kept his lips shut tight against the fierce wind, stopped us even whispering amongst ourselves. Consequently our midnight flit was conducted in silence, except for our suffering friend's groans. But whenever the truck's headlamps illuminated the dark tree-lined valley as if reflected by rising river water, or shone over the peaks in the wake of the night beasts' cries which suddenly rose up in the depths of the forest, we peered keen-eyed for the deserter who might be in hiding there.

Then the long journey's fatigue, our pointless excitement, the truck's vibration and the MP's supervision merged and pulled us into a deep sleep, and we pressed our heads down on the hard, rough boards. Since he had dozed off straight away, I cradled my brother's handsome head in my arms to protect his childlike slumber, but as I did so I too fell asleep, lying across his body.

When I opened my eyes, awakened by the chattering murmur of my uneasy slumber and the arm shaking me, I groaned loudly at this unpleasant reveille which had become almost routine thanks to the frequent air raids. I found myself stretched out on the planking with my brother trying to shake me fully awake. The others had all got out of the truck, and the villager, stretching his short body, was having trouble disentangling the bicycle's front wheel from the back end of the truck. I jumped up quickly, dusted down my clothes and pushed at the bicycle's cold and wet handlebars to give him a hand. The bicycle was quite heavy, and the man gave me a dull, amiable smile over my straining and trembling arms. When he put the bicycle on the ground I jumped down, but my brother hesitated. Then the villager's strong arms effortlessly lifted him down, as he laughed bashfully, tickled.

'Thanks,' said my brother, in a low voice befitting a new-forged friendship.

'Yah,' said the villager, taking hold of the bicycle.

Beyond the mass of dark night air, behind the looming stretch of pale narrow road was a bonfire with many people crowded round it. The MPs and the warden went over. The villager followed them, bouncing awkwardly on his bicycle. We huddled by the side of the truck, the backs of our necks goose-pimpled from the cold, and watched them. It was cold. It was a strange cold, a new cold that sunk deep into the core of our being, as if we had entered an utterly different climate. We've really gone into the mountains, I thought. We shivered like dogs, miserably pressing our thin shoulders together. That was also because of a stiff tension which ringed that bonfire site like forest trees, provoking a subtle sympathetic resonance in our group. I silently watched the MPs and the warden go in amongst the villagers and start their discussions.

The villagers surrounded the MPs and the warden and conferred hastily, but their deliberations didn't reach our desperately straining ears. With our eyes grown used to the darkness, we could see, by intermittent flares when the bonfire blazed up, a number of army cadets and the slow movements of villagers who were carrying bamboo spears and hoes. It was like a little war going on over there. We watched it, our bodies tense.

The middle-aged villager returned from the circle of arguing adults, firewood piled on the rear rack of his bicycle. He flung the wood off it and went back in silence: this time he came clutching a green branch which was blazing vigorously and spurting sap. As he propped the bicycle against a tree, we heaped the wood up and started a fire. The wood hardly burned at all. We dashed warily into the sparse forest and carried out armfuls of dried leaves and carefully arranged dead twigs, which snapped easily with a sharp sound, round the fire. As the villager thrust his head into the smoke, nurturing the flames with abandon, traces of countless burns showed on his heavily tanned ochre bull neck with every spasmodic expansion and contraction of the small blaze, that fat neck with its lifeless dried-up stoutness and appearance.

When our bonfire started to crackle gently and a steady smoke began to rise, we and the villager began to feel a sense of togetherness from the work of making the fire. Moreover, because the blood quickened and was flowing under our chilled flesh, producing an itchy glow, we couldn't help relaxing. It was the same for the villager. For no reason, we stood smiling round the sweet-smelling bonfire, which now burned fiercely.

'Mister, are you a blacksmith?' my brother asked in a

shy voice. 'Eh, are you?'

'Yah,' said the villager happily. 'I could forge sickles when I was your age.'

'Great,' said my brother in open admiration. 'Could I do it too?'

'It's a question of practice,' said the villager. 'You saw my bicycle? I rebuilt the pedals, made them stronger.' The blacksmith got up, took his bicycle out from under the tree, laid it across his lap before our admiring eyes, and gave a short laugh as he traced with the cracked ball of his thumb the overthick axis of the pedal, clumsy and angular yet looking like a limb just as a hoe or sickle did, and the worn-out crank arm.

'I didn't know blacksmiths rebuilt bicycles,' said my brother.

'Of course you didn't,' said the smith, as he laid his bicycle down on the black earth that steamed from the bonfire's heat and thrust two or three sticks of firewood into the flames. 'No one knows that,' he added.

Listening to the sound of erupting sap, the quiet motion of the air, the sound of clumps of ash falling, the villager's laughter lingering in his throat, we thought in silence about the reformatory's one and only bicycle. Now it must be leaning against the inside wall, the perished rubber of its mudstained tyres cracking. . .

A mighty din rose up around the other bonfire. A man with a penetrating voice was giving orders. Lifting our heads and peering into the thick darkness, we could see the men over there starting to form up in line.

'They're army cadets, aren't they?' one of us asked the blacksmith. 'Are they all here on exercise, or are they looking for the deserter?'

'Ah,' the blacksmith replied readily to his question. 'They're hunting in the mountains. Not just the cadets, they and the villagers are all hunting together. We've run around the mountains for three days without seeing anything. If the soldier bolted this way, he'd hit a dead end. The only way to get to our village on the other side of the valley is by trolley. No one can cross the valley 'cos of the flood. The thing is, we searched through this area but can't find him. We're going to call off the hunt and go home to the other side of the valley. The soldier must have drowned at the bottom of the valley.'

Hunting: the silent night hunt of villagers bearing spears and hoes; the soldier pursued, running through the woods and drowning in the flooded valley. We sighed deeply, plunged in the bloody image of hunting which shook our bodies. We were really in the maelstrom of war. And a stupefying crisis, like a beast, was nosing its dark head towards us. Ah, hunting.

'That must've been awful,' I said. 'Hunting, that must've been awful.'

'It's terrible. Worse than boar hunting,' said the blacksmith. 'The villagers running and beating the bushes for three days without eating or drinking.' Despite those bitter words, he showed a cheerful countenance in the bright glare of the bonfire. He repeated himself very slowly, the glittering reflections of the flames sparkling on his thick wet lips. 'It's terrible; covered with scratches all over your body, and even so not even a rabbit comes out.'

'Do you catch rabbits with that sort of hunting?' said my brother in obvious surprise. 'And hares?'

'If they come out, we catch them,' said the blacksmith earnestly. 'Pigeons, pheasants, and rabbits.'

As my brother leaned forward, intending to bombard the blacksmith with questions about his beloved small animals, the warden and a strapping villager came briskly over to our bonfire. Closing his mouth and hugging his knees, the blacksmith indicated that the conversation was at an end, and we stiffened once more.

'Here's the village headman who'll take care of you. Stand up and bow,' said the warden, in a relieved voice. 'That's right.'

We stood watching the big man with his sharp chin, who wore thick cotton work clothes and a fur hat that covered his ears. He stared back at us with eyes whose lower lids sagged; eyes, however, that shone with a sharp brown glint.

'The arrangements for your reception have been ready for three days,' the headman said, moving his jaw with its coarse protruding bristles as if he were chewing grain. 'You can relax.'

'I'm entrusting you to the headman here,' said the warden. 'I've decided to catch a lift in the army truck and go back to escort the second party. You, behave yourselves. All right?'

The headman's voice resounded over our collective assent.

'We villagers'll think of what to do, depending on your attitude.'

'Don't make any trouble: group leader, make a note if anyone breaks the rules. I'll punish them when the evacuation's completed.'

This kind of procedure hung over us all the time, fettering and retarding our actions and pulling us down into a heavy confusion of irritation and fatigue. Handing over the list of names, the roll call; nominating the group leader; after that a feeble chorus of the reformatory song; dirty-faced farmers with torn coats, clutching weapons, gradually gathering inquisitively round our hunger-wracked company. We were all shabby, jittery and keyed up.

The cadets came marching in line from the other bonfire to get into the truck. We watched them while the truck turned round with a screeching noise, but they were tired, faces heavy with despondency, sullenly silent, no longer youthful or beautiful. They too had run round mountain paths after rain, round the valley pockmarked with landslides, on the hunt, and their lusty, sturdy, animal beauty was dissipated.

We left the army cadets and the warden boarding the truck, and went up the steep, narrow mountain path, shepherded by the silent farmers armed with bamboo spears and hoes. Dark bushes closed in on us and lacerated our frozen flesh, drawing blood from our fingers, from our cheeks, from the skin between our earlobes and the napes of our necks. As the din from the truck died away we heard a violent sound of water coming from the depths of the night forest and, pricking up our ears, hurried headlong on. The villagers' silence infected us and, through the forest, on the high cliffs of the valley where a cold hard wind blew up, and even when we came out onto a narrow, level stone ledge, none of us tried to say a word.

At the end of the dark stone ledge there was a solid timber frame which caught the dim light. And there was a trolley for transporting logs standing on a track which stretched across the valley. Following the headman's instructions, we boarded it.

'Don't move, don't move at all,' the headman warned us repeatedly after shouting a signal to the winch operator, who seemed to be on the other side of the valley. 'If anyone moves you'll all tip over and die. Don't move, don't move at all.'

His heavy, vexed voice fell over us like the buzzing of insects, accumulated on our dirt-encrusted bodies and mingled with the faint sound of water which rose from the deep, dark valley bottom. We waited for the departure in the trolley's narrow, lime-caked skip, sitting motionless, piled dog-tired on top of each other like strays caught by the dog-catcher. Don't move, don't move at all. If anyone moves you'll all tip over and die. Don't move, don't move at all.

Then the trolley started. Carrying us, it advanced slowly along the track across the deep valley, trembling softly, advancing into an intense stifling miasma of tree bark and buds, into the expanse of forest on the far side, darker than the valley floor. And the winter night's dry, hard air wrapped itself tightly around the skip sliding along the narrow unstable track, the youngsters wedged in inside, and the wire rope hauling them.

I stretched my arm between jam-packed bodies, groping for and finding my brother's small soft palm and squeezed it tightly. The warmth of his fingers squeezing back with all his frail strength, the youthful pulse sent back to me a nimble, resilient vitality, like a rabbit or squirrel. That feeling must have also been conveyed from my palm to his. I was scared, an anxiety that set my lips trembling and fatigue spreading all over my body, then flowing from my hand to my brother's; and it must have been the same for him. Loaded like dogs that had lost the will to resist, exposing ourselves to this dangerous transit, we stuck it out, chewing our lips in fear.

Adult voices shouting in a rough dialect, apparently exasperated, resounded sporadically from both sides of the valley and echoed around the valley floor. But they made no sense to us. Everything except the swelling, rich odour of the night forest and the squeaking of the track raged far above our small, drooping heads like the sound of a storm wind at night.

The boy who had suffered from stomach-ache throughout our long march to the valley started groaning again behind his chattering teeth. He struggled to endure the gut-wrenching pain without moving, and groaned in a feeble voice.

'Hey, don't throw up on my shoulder,' Minami said coldly.

The groaning voice was muffled, and its owner said, ah, as if sighing. I saw his small pale face with his hand pressed over his mouth against the piled-up bodies of our comrades and lowered my eyes again. What could we do about it? We had to stay put until the carriage loaded with boys had crossed the valley.

Then at last, when the trolley stopped with a slight bang, a young farmer, straddling the cable that wound round a thick timber axle, shouted at us as he pushed a wooden chock home.

'Here you are. Get out, quick.'

Chapter Two:
The First Little Task

Surrounded by the silent villagers clutching their weapons, we went down the narrow sloping path into the damp dark forest. The sound of frozen bark cracking deep in the forest, the rustling of small beasts' stealthy flight, the shrill cries and sudden wingbeats of birds assaulted us and often made us cringe in alarm. The night forest was like a quietly raging sea. The villagers hemmed us in, front and back, as if we were prisoners of war, though there was no need. Not even our most reckless boys had the courage to dash into that vast forest, which raged and grew calm like a sea. After passing through the forest, the road stretched away in the pallid darkness, spread with small stones rounded by rain and wind that felt pleasant underfoot, making the descent easier. Then, further on, spread out along a narrow curved valley, there was a small village.

The houses were crowded together, shut in gloomily next to each other like trees in the black valley. They huddled together in silence like night beasts, ranged from the valley's low rim to its deep hollow, interspersed with gaps then running on again. A vague emotion grew in our breasts as we stopped and looked down on them.

'They've put out the lights because of the blackout,' the headman explained to us. 'Your billet is a little up from that group of houses, in the temple to the right of the fire tower.'

Straining our eyes, we saw, on the even darker rise that was the beginning of the slope leading up to the mountain directly opposite, a short squat iron-framed tower that merged into the forest behind like a tree, then we looked down to its right at a one-storey building larger than the village houses in the bottom of the valley and, facing that, another large two-storey building. The two-storey building was surrounded by several smaller adjoining houses and beyond by clay walls. We gazed at the pale gleam of the low clay walls.

'I want to live on that top floor,' said my brother, and laughter burst out amongst the villagers beside us. It was full of hidden strength and meant to be mocking.

'Your billet,' repeated the headman, 'is the one-storey building facing that. Understand?'

'Ah,' my brother said, plainly disappointed. 'I thought as much.'

We walked on, and the village was obscured by the shadows of the old trees which loomed over both sides of the paved road, cutting out the sky. After that we had to walk for a long time. Then finally we went down into the valley, which turned out to be unexpectedly large and intricate, with a handful of pale plots of unharvested frost-blighted vegetables shimmering between the houses.

With their wooden doors shut, the houses seemed fast asleep, but straight away we noticed beady eyes peering round half-closed doors and from corners of windows, and we had to lower our eyes to ignore them. Dogs were barking.

At the foot of the incline our procession changed direction, leaving almost half the villagers behind, and went up a narrow sharply sloping path past an open well, through a stench of mouldy old rubbish that crammed itself into our nostrils, and came out on another paved road. On the left was an open space and a building with many windows.

'That's the village school,' said the headman. 'It's closed now. The roads from the town have been washed away in the flood. The teachers won't come. We had to close it.'

We were too tired to take an interest in the school, the lazy teachers and the village children pleased with their long, unexpected holiday. We walked on in silence, hanging our heads. As we climbed up the slope there was a warehouse-like structure, then came a solidly constructed building, different from the rickety and beastly shabby houses flanking the road we had passed along, surrounded by walls broken by short flights of stone steps. Further on there was a temple with a narrow garden and eaves deep enough to shut out the sky. Standing in line in the garden, we went through the petty and minutely detailed procedure for entering new quarters: don't light fires on the premises; don't dirty the toilets; to begin with meals will be supplied by the villagers. We received these admonitions and went through it all, nodding obediently.

'Your job is to clear the mountain fields, don't shirk,'

the headman suddenly shouted in a rough voice at the end of his speech. 'Anyone caught stealing, starting fires or making a row will be beaten to death by the villagers. Don't forget that you're vermin here. Even so, we'll shelter and feed you. Always remember that in this village you're only useless vermin.'

We stood in the cold dark garden, tired youngsters sopping up sleep like a sponge sucking up water, so beaten down we could not even speak. What was more, before going indoors we had to wash our feet and submit to a physical examination.

When the last villager had left, we squatted in darkness, since he had turned off the bare electric bulb. We were groping with salt-and-saliva-coated fingers for the coarse potatoes in the bamboo basket, and stoically got on with our late-night meal. We went on eating the already cold and sweaty potatoes in silence, feeling a gritty stagnation at the back of our mouths.

How poor was the meal that was given to us, that awaited us at the end of our long journey. Three basketfuls of scrawny potatoes and a handful of hard rock salt. We were disappointed and angry. But as there was nothing else we could do, we went on patiently eating. We were sitting surrounded by white walls and thick crossbeams on the damp tatami of the sanctuary, which was partitioned off from the narrow earth-floored entrance and the toilet by a wooden door. Just by sitting there, we made the interior stuffy. There were no other rooms in that building, and no villagers living there either.

There were still some potatoes left, but at last our

stomachs would not accept any more coarse food, and sleep and a vague sorrow which came from satisfaction soaked like water into our soft heads. One by one we left the baskets, wiped our fingers on the seat of our pants, then lay down on our backs, sharing the thin blankets between us. Our eyes, adjusted to the dark, began to make out the crossbeams through the murky air.

The groans of the boy who had suffered from stomachache throughout the journey filled the cramped interior, but none of us paid any attention to him. We strained our eyes and pricked up our ears in the darkness. Mysterious beasts' cries, sounds of splitting bark, the surging noise caused by the wind's sudden passage: they beat at us from outside.

My brother sat up abruptly from his sleeping posture with his forehead pressed against my back. He hesitated for a moment.

'What?' I said in a low muffled voice.

'I'm thirsty,' he said, his voice husky and nervous. 'There was a well in the garden. I want to go and get a drink.'

'I'll go with you.'

'It's all right,' he said in a feverish tone, his feelings clearly hurt. 'I'm not scared.'

Having half risen, I lay down again and heard him go down onto the earth floor and try to open the low door that led outside. He seemed to be having trouble. He repeated his futile efforts a few times, then after tut-tutting, came back to me, plainly at a loss.

'It's locked from the outside,' he said, disappointed. 'I don't know what to do.'

'It's locked?' said Minami in a loud voice which charged the air in the room with tension. 'I'll smash it down.'

He jumped down on the earth floor and attacked the low door violently, but against our expectations he only spat out filthy abuse. We heard the sound of Minami boldly hurling himself against the low door and repeatedly bouncing back. He couldn't manage it.

'Bastards,' Minami said angrily, after slowly climbing back from the earth floor and burrowing beneath his comrade's blanket. 'They want to keep us shut in. They won't let us drink and just give us the same ration of potatoes as they give their pigs.'

Thirst choked us like a common fit. The saliva began to thicken in our mouths, our tongues paralyzed by pain. We had to sleep. Only it was terribly cold. And more, thirst clutched at us. We were using all the strength in our tired bodies just to keep the sobs from rising and bursting out in throats already numbed by a terrible thirst.

Next morning, watched by the village men who had come to open the wooden door from the outside, the village women who had carried in the food wrapped in rough cloth, and the village children who peered at us as they skulked behind trees and corners of walls, we ate hard brown rice balls, crammed vegetable stew into our mouths with our fingers and drank tea from red copper containers. It was neither good food, nor sufficient. But we ate it in silence.

After the meal, the blacksmith came up the slope with a hunting rifle on his shoulder and the other villagers left. But the children, watching us eagerly, didn't even try to move. When we waved our arms and shouted at them, they kept stubbornly silent, their earth-coloured faces blank and expressionless.

The blacksmith looked us up and down for a moment in a calculating fashion. Then he went over to the boy who had been weakened since the night before by stomach-ache and hadn't even touched the food brought to his bedside. As our silent scrutiny focused on the blacksmith bending over and studying our exhausted young comrade, he looked back over his broad shoulder, a bemused half-smile playing round his lips.

'Apart from this one, you've all got work to do.'

'Work?' I said.

'You're going to make us work this morning?' Minami cried jokingly. 'Let's have a rest today.'

'What you'll do today,' replied the blacksmith, flustered, 'isn't what you'd call work. You'll just bury a few little things.'

'Bury what?' asked my brother, his curiosity stirring.

'Don't answer back each time,' the indignant blacksmith retorted. 'Get outside and form a line.'

Bustling, we tied our shoelaces and rushed out into the garden. The blacksmith went on talking to the prostrate boy; then, when he hurried out, we followed him down the slope. The village children came running after us in a swarm, but kept their distance. When we turned and made threatening gestures they retreated immediately, only to come trailing behind once more, observing us warily.

It was morning; it was a fine winter morning. The middle of the road which was covered in crushed stones, the centre stretch that rose in a hog's back, was dry and threw up dust, but pillars of ice, which creaked then collapsed suddenly as we stepped on them, remained on both verges where dried yellow-stemmed weeds sprawled. And the cold, which bore a slight stink of frozen horse dung, pierced the air all around like arrows.

At the bottom of the slope, there was a slightly wider road paved with rounded brick-sized stones and small low houses. They were what we had seen last night through the dark air. But now they were drenched in morning sun, and the thatched roofs and earth walls threw back a soft golden lustre. The mountains that had scared us during the night, the sparse forest traversed by the road from the valley, and the steeply sloping arc of woodland ranged beside it that surrounded the village, overflowed with blue light and pale brown sheen, and birdsong surged up from all sides. Our spirits began to rise little by little, then suddenly swelled, and we almost wanted to sing. We had arrived at the village where we were going to spend the remainder of the winter and several seasons after that, and we were ready for work. It would be good to work. Up till now the only work we had been given was roughing out toys, or pointlessly planting pot-atoes in barren ground, or at best making wooden-soled sandals. The silence of the blacksmith, who hurried along bent over, had an air of honest toil. We flared our nostrils in expectation, sucked in the cold air and trembled.

'There's a dead dog,' shouted my brother. 'Look, it's only a puppy.'

We walked into a thicket of weeds at the base of a low apricot tree which my brother had run to, and saw it.

'This one got killed by a bad stomach.' As he shouted, turning his flushed cheeks to face us, a couple of the younger boys ran up. 'Its stomach's swollen.'

'Hey,' the blacksmith yelled, still expressionless, waving

his arm senselessly at them. 'Don't break ranks without permission.'

My brother and his companions, evidently flustered, made to get back in line. I felt that he couldn't hide his ill feeling at the betrayal of last night's friendship with the blacksmith.

'Come here and drag that dog along,' the smith said vaguely, treating him with particular favouritism. We laughed, and my brother was puzzled. But the blacksmith earnestly repeated his order.

'Hitch a length of rope round it and drag it.'

My brother no longer hesitated, but quickly picked up a stiff, frozen length of rope from the grass and bent over the dead dog. Raising a cheer, the younger boys went to give him a hand.

'They'll roast it and make us eat it,' Minami said in a low voice, with comical gloom. 'It's going to be awful.'

'You even eat cats,' I said. 'Rats or anything.'

'There's a dead cat here,' he said in a slightly stunned voice. Sure enough, a cat's fluffy delicate hind legs were peeping out from the knotted grass at his feet. 'It's a spotty cat.'

'Drag that one along too,' the blacksmith said calmly. 'Don't hang around.'

With a vaguely choked feeling, we tied the swollen-bellied lock-jawed corpses of the dog and cat together with the rope and dragged them along.

We went down the narrow lane overgrown with grass where a little dirty snow still lay beside the primitive school building. From there on a steep slope led down to the narrow valley which closed like the bottom of a bag. And there was some sort of open tunnel like an abandoned mine shaft in the small rise opposite, and a cluster of shabby little houses.

We tripped down the slope into the valley.

Where the narrow lane disappeared into the meadow sodden with melted frost, we noticed a shed and a byre. The blacksmith thrust a shoulder through the entrance of the shed, which was built of rough-hewn logs, and shouted.

'Has anything gone at your place?'

'Not a single one,' said a low thick voice. There were sounds of someone getting up inside the dark shed. 'So far, not one.'

'I'll borrow your hoes.'

'Yeah.'

The blacksmith went into the earthen entrance and came back carrying several hoes which he threw down on the damp ground. These were hoes for use in the mountains, fitted with thick dull iron heads on short thick handles: very hefty hoes. We scrambled to pick them up and shoulder them. It thrilled us and filled us with pride to be given tools; even more, to be given solid and manly agricultural implements like real people.

But the blacksmith's behaviour towards us wasn't quite appropriate for real people. He held his gun ready and carefully aimed it at us as we picked up and shouldered the tools. The villager came out of the shed and looked at us and the corpses we had dragged along without changing expression at all. We were a little struck by his impassivity, but the flabby skin beneath his eyes like bags of rheum looked as if it might swell up, close his eyes and send him to sleep.

'Is that all for this morning?' the man said slowly, as if bored.

''It'll be your cow next,' said the blacksmith.

'If the cow goes, that's it,' said the man indignantly. 'I mean if my cow goes, that's it.'

The blacksmith shook his head and signalled us to go down to the meadow. He was careful not to take the lead and turn his back on us while we carried the tools that could be used as weapons. We ran down to the end of the valley where its narrow river was glimmering in the sun. A slight breeze, heavier and thicker than the air in the village, was circulating there, bringing a little warmth.

We turned round and looked up the valley slope. The village children were coming down quickly behind the blacksmith and the village houses were perched on the slope like a flock of birds when we looked up to the cold hard blue sky. The blacksmith signalled us to move to the right, waving his arm violently. We walked against rough-stemmed herbs scratching our skin, and mud and hairy seeds of leguminous grasses stuck to the stiffened limbs of the carcasses that were as motionless as plants.

Then we suddenly stopped short before a heaped-up mound of strange objects, breathing hard, in our heavy shoes that were filthy from tramping in mud.

Dogs, cats, fieldmice, goats, even foals; scores of animal carcasses were piled up forming a small hill, quietly and patiently decomposing. The beasts' teeth were clenched, their pupils melting, their legs stiff. Their dead flesh and blood had turned into thick mucus making the yellow withered grass and mud around sticky, and — strangely full of life and holding out against the fierce onslaught of decay — there were countless ears.

Fat winter flies fell upon the animals like black snow, regularly rising up a little, and made a music filled with silence that flooded our heads. We reeled from shock.

'Ah,' my brother sighed. Before these piled-up beasts' carcasses, the red dog which he had dragged with the rope seemed as meaningless and common as grass or earth.

'Dig a hole and bury them,' said the blacksmith. 'Don't stand around gawping; work!'

But we only stood there vacantly, in a stench which we could smell with the skin of our faces, never mind our nostrils, like a thick liquid gushing out from the mass of beasts. The stink which gushed out , twisting and twining, was impregnated with something that tantalized us. Children who have sniffed eagerly with their small noses pressed up against the hindquarters of a bitch in heat, children who have the courage and the reckless desire to enjoy, even for a short while, the dangerous pleasure of rapidly stroking the back of an aroused dog, can recognize the subtle human signal and allure in the stink of animal carcasses. We opened our eyes wide, fit to burst, and inhaled lustily.

'There's another one here,' a voice called behind us, timid and bashful yet imperious, in a clipped rural dialect.

We turned around and saw one of the village children who had gathered on a mound a short distance away, dangling a small rat with a swollen belly between his fingertips.

'You fool. Don't touch it! Remember?' shouted the blacksmith, the veins standing out on his throat. 'Go home and wash your hands.'

Trembling, the boy flicked the baby rat away and ran up

the slope leading to the village. Bewildered, we watched the blacksmith follow the village child with his eyes, his face burning with righteous anger.

'Go and pick that up,' he said, stifling his anger.

But none of us tried to go and pick it up. We scented a strange omen in the rat.

'Go and get it, eh?' said the blacksmith, softening his tone.

I started running. Once the village children had screamed and run away, I crouched and picked up the hard, shrunken rat's tail between finger and thumb and went back. Ignoring the reproach in my brother's eyes, I threw the rat on top of the mountain of beasts which continued their endless mute call. The rat bounced off the back of a hairless cat bleached from exposure to the rain, slid down other animals and slipped under the naked protruding buttocks of a goat. A wave of laughter rose in our group, immediately relieving the tension.

'Well, go on,' said the blacksmith, encouraged.

Wielding the hoes, we dug up the brown earth matted with withered grass and dead leaves. The surface was soft and yielded easily. When fat orange-white larvae, hibernating frogs and shrews were unearthed, they were immediately struck and killed by our well-aimed hoes. The thin fog soaking the valley quickly cleared, but the piled-up animal carcasses filled the air with a stench that never faded, like another fog in its wake.

We were digging a rectangular hole of exactly two metres by three. After the soft layer, a slightly harder layer containing white crystalline pebbles appeared. And whenever the hoes struck, cold water oozed out. Pale winter sunshine made our cheeks and foreheads sweat. As the hole grew deeper, fewer people could work in it. I threw down my hoe and wiped the sweat from my forehead. The village children nervously drew closer once more. But when they saw me stop working, they got ready to run. I noticed a girl, the scruff of her neck blackened with grime, and her pouting lips, button nose and sickly watery eyes robbed me of the pleasure of scaring them. In the villages we had passed through on our journey, I had frightened enough girls of that type to grow sick of it. When the girls squatted to urinate, baring their small scraggy bums, we would pounce on them suddenly, yelling. But going on with that game held no more interest for us. I really loathed and despised the village children.

'Hey, don't slack,' the blacksmith shouted, coming nearer.

'Ah,' I said, starting work. 'That hunting rifle's got a big bore.'

'It's a gun for bear; it'll bring down men too,' the blacksmith said menacingly, drawing the gun back from my outstretched hand. 'If you give me any trouble, I'll shoot you dead. For us it's nothing to kill you.'

'I know,' I said, hurt. 'If the village children touched a dead rat, they'd get germs. If we touch them, it doesn't matter. Right?'

'Eh?' the flustered blacksmith stammered.

'An animal plague's broken out?' I asked, pointing with my chin towards my comrades who had started dumping the animal carcasses into the newly-dug hole. 'What sort of plague is it?'

'How should I know?' said the blacksmith craftily. 'The doctor doesn't know either.'

'It doesn't matter if the animals die. The worst it can do is kill a horse?' I asked even more craftily than the blacksmith, and my question caught him out.

'People died too,' he said in one breath.

'A Korean died,' shouted a village boy whose curiosity had conquered his fear, sticking his head out from behind the blacksmith. 'Look, a flag's gone up, hasn't it?'

We looked up at a group of unbelievably shabby houses clumped on the mountainside beyond the valley. A faded vermilion paper flag was fluttering in the wind on one of the outermost houses. There was no windflow in the valley, but halfway up the mountain there must be a wind blowing all day, smelling of earth and new leaves. Up there, you would find no smell of rotting dogs. . .

'Over there?' The shy village boy shut his mouth tight as I asked in reply. 'A Korean died over there?'

'It's the Korean settlement; only one man died,' the blacksmith answered instead of the child. 'We don't know whether it was the same illness as the beasts or not.'

My comrades were trying to carry a heavy calf whose stomach had burst, decanting pulpy flesh, blood and body fluids. It seemed that the virulent disease which had attacked the strong calf could also easily attack humans.

'A woman evacuee is half dead in the warehouse,' another child shrilled in excitement. 'Because she picked up a rotten vegetable and ate it; everybody says so.'

'If it's plague, you have to put her in an isolation hospital. It's awful when it starts to spread. It'll kill everyone.'

'There's no isolation hospital,' said the blacksmith morosely. 'We don't have that sort of thing.'

'When the plague's going round the village, what do you do?' I persisted.

'The whole village'll run away. We escape and leave the sick. That's the rule. When plague breaks out in our village, the neighbouring villages take care of us. Contrariwise, if the plague breaks out in other villages, we feed those who've escaped to our village. Twenty years ago, when cholera broke out, we stayed in the next village for three months.'

Twenty years ago: it had the solemn simplicity of a legend and made me imagine. Twenty years ago, in the darkness of history, the villagers had taken flight, abandoning the groaning, suffering victims. This survivor, close enough for me to smell his body odour, is talking to me.

'Why don't you escape this time?' I asked, unable to stop gasping.

'Eh?' he said. 'This time? The plague hasn't spread too far. The animals died, two people fell ill, one died. That's all.'

And the blacksmith shut his mouth tight, tensing his lips and turned his face away from me. I ran back and joined my comrades' labours. We carried various animals, including the tiny dog, and threw them down on top of the others that were packed tight in the hole. Most of the animals were rotting, and when the skin on their hindquarters came off in my hands I felt the germs from the beasts attack me in a swarm with horrible force, and a cold sweat ran down my back. But by the time my sense of smell had been numbed by the stink, that feeling had vanished from my consciousness. And when we looked up impatiently as we finished carrying the animals and laid earth over them, the sun was shining in the narrow sky hemmed in on both sides by mountains, and the full light of noon was pouring precipitously down.

'When lunch is over, we'll pack down the earth,' said the blacksmith. 'Go and wash your hands carefully in the river.'

Cheering, we ran down to the narrow river in the valley bottom, waving our mud-caked arms. There were velvety stones covered with dried moss and a trickle of clear water running between them; when we put our fingers in it, a fierce pain ran through our bodies. But as we rubbed our fingers, red, swollen and paralyzed with cold, little rainbows briefly appeared between them and the sun's pulsating glitter made happy laughter rise up in our throats.

'Wash carefully, there's loads of germs,' I said in a loud voice. 'If someone who hasn't washed touches you, you'll get the plague.'

'Dog's disease, rat's disease,' Minami shouted jokily, spashing the water. 'Cat's disease, beetle's disease.'

We all laughed loudly and yelled at each other, but one of the boys suddenly shut his mouth, tensed his cheeks and peered through the water's surface. His silence immediately infected everyone and, piled on each others' backs, we gazed at what his trembling finger was pointing to.

'It's a crab,' my brother cried in amazement.

It was a crab. Through the pale sky-coloured water, on tawny sand, the armoured legs of a crab the size of a child's palm were peeping out between the rocks. Brown hairs on the ridges along each leg were waving in the current. My brother gingerly dipped his hand into the water and brought it close to the crab's legs. Then perhaps a finger touched it, for immediately the water clouded in a swirl of earth and sand, and when it had cleared not a thing remained behind. We laughed hoarsely and inhaled the river's smell, the normal smell of water and sand, through our refreshed noses.

'Come here, come here, what are you doing?' the blacksmith was shouting in irritation.

On our way back to the temple, climbing the slope, trampling the withered grass, then going along the stone-paved village street, our march was obstructed by the villagers who were gathered in front of the warehouse-like building. Peering intently through the warehouse's open doorway, they paid our stalled procession no attention. The village children ran timidly past us and went in among the adults' group. From the interior of the warehouse came a young girl's sobbing that choked us all up.

A man with an extraordinarily bald forehead and large protruding ears came out of the warehouse doorway carrying a bulging old leather bag. When he shook his head hard, an anxious murmur ran among the villagers and several of them went into the warehouse.

'How's it going, doctor?' the blacksmith said, his voice rising unnaturally in the villagers' gloomy silence.

'Well . . . ,' the man said superciliously, not answering the blacksmith's question directly, and pushed his way through the villagers towards us.

He looked us over carefully. It wasn't pleasant to be stared at by that man's tired, brown, muddy eyes, and the uncanny feeling of what he had left behind shut up in the warehouse came through him to intimidate us.

'Who's the leader?' said the man in a low rough voice. 'Your leader.'

Horribly flustered, egged on and urged by my comrades' eyes, I stammered a reply.

'Me, but it doesn't really matter who.'

'Ah?' the man said. 'I saw your sick friend. Maybe tomorrow, come to the next village to get medicine. I'll draw you a map.'

He took a notebook out of the bulging bag, drew a detailed map in it with a pencil, then tore out the page and pressed it into my outstretched hand. Before thrusting it into my breast pocket I tried to read it, just to make sure, but the simple map conveyed no clear meaning to me.

As I tried to ask the man, who seemed to be a doctor, about our comrade's condition, the headman came out of the warehouse holding the sobbing girl and led her off up the slope. The girl's wailing, as though her skin was burning all over her body, shocked us into silence like dumb animals.

Chapter Three:

The Plague's Onslaught and the Villagers' Exodus

In the afternoon we were going to pack down the earth of the hole the animals were buried in. Finishing our plain food, we waited for a long time seated on the narrow temple verandah, catching the weak winter sun on our tired bodies, but the blacksmith who had directed our labours didn't come back up the slope beyond the garden. And the village children, whose expressions changed little and who were completely filthy, stood with their arms folded and gazed attentively at us. When we threatened them, they would scatter in panic like dogs but would quickly reassemble again. We soon became bored with this one-sided game of tag and, ignoring them like trees and grass, devoted ourselves to our own games. After all, it was our first rest since we came to the village.

Some of us tidied our kit-bags, laying out our valuables — mysterious tubes or bronze handles, bloodstained lengths of chain for use as weapons and pieces of bulletproof glass — in the sunshine and polishing them with cloths. Others concentrated on finishing a model plane carved from a block of soft wood. Minami had to treat his anus, chronically inflamed as a result of his self-sacrificial passion. He made his obedient sidekick rub on some of the small amount of ointment left in the celluloid container that he took out from his kit-bag. He had to assume a humiliating position like a small animal defecating to treat the affected area, but if anybody mocked him he would jump up straight away with his trousers down and strike his insolent foe. We were at ease and, for the first time in the last couple of days, we spent the afternoon in idleness. Only the boy who had suffered from stomachache during the journey, too weak by now even to groan, lay prostrate with his face upturned. But what could we do about it?

All at once the air grew cold, a wind blew up and the dusk rose from the treetops which shut out the light to the low sky. Then the silent village women brought the evening meal, and after our hurried dinner all the wooden doors were shut again and locked from the outside. The blacksmith, who was present at our meal, kept silent, his face set hard, and would not be drawn by our leading questions. Once we were imprisoned by ourselves inside the dark temple, a peculiar smell from the morning's work that had soaked into our bodies, our clothes and above all our spirits gradually rose up and merged into the room's stale air. Despite it, we tried to call up sleep before our eyes and inside ourselves, oppressed as we were by the fatigue which filled our bodies, as we lay buried beneath the heavy atmosphere.

But our sick comrade's weak, fitful breathing and the cries of animals in the night forest and the cracking of trees outside the wooden door snatched at us, and we could hardly get to sleep. Besides, signs of movement, a stirring of stealthy and stifled pleasure arose here and there, but I myself was too tired to indulge in it.

Later that night our long-suffering comrade died. At that instant we suddenly awoke. It was not that we were affected by any harsh noise and sudden sense of presence; it was rather the complete opposite. In our shallow sleep, one quiet sound vanished and one being was lost. That strangely different feeling caught us all together. We sat up in the darkness. Suddenly the weak sobbing of one of the younger boys shook the dark air. Tearfully, he told us of the catastrophe that had befallen our friend. We understood immediately. Groping in the dark, we gathered around the dead boy, now rapidly beginning to turn cold and stiff, who only at nightfall had still been our comrade. We elbowed aside each other's warm bodies and touched the flesh which had lost its vital heat, then drew our arms back as if recoiling.

Suddenly a couple of us started shouting, clinging to the wooden door that led to the outside. That infected us all and set off a general panic. We yelled and banged on the door, pressing our bodies against it, as if we wanted to be as far as possible from the corpse.

'Hey! Hey! Come on, open up! Hey! The sick boy's died.'

'Hey! Hey!' we cried, but our chorus of voices carried no clear meaning, like the cries of beasts in the night forest. Then we felt as if only grief poured out its radiance from that pushing and jostling, those confused voices, spreading to the sky and the depths of the valley.

After a long time had passed and our cries had grown weak and dull with fatigue and hoarseness, we heard the agitated footsteps of a crowd coming up the road in front of the garden, and the lock on the wooden door made a heavy sound. We fell silent and waited. But before entering, the villagers hesitated and shone a flashlight in from outside the door. In front of me I saw my brother's dazzling face, stained with tears. Then I saw the headman and the blacksmith enter, aiming their guns from the hip and watching us warily. We kept silent. And we breathed harshly. They were as tense as armed wardens quelling a prison riot, biting their lips and flaring their nostrils.

'What is it, you brats?' growled the headman. 'Making such a noise; what's the matter?'

I tried to explain the situation, swallowing my saliva to loosen my hoarse throat, but there was no need. The beam from the flashlight which the blacksmith swung in his left hand caught the deceased and settled on him. They approached our dead comrade, their boots squarely on the matting and, under our silent scrutiny, their features tensed suspiciously. Then they bent over, holding the flashlight, and examined the body. In the circle of wan yellow light, there was a pale, scruffy, tiny head, the stiffened skin like a fruit rind, and under the nose a smear of dried blood. And heavy eyelids peeled back by rough fingers, and arms folded one on top of the other around his stomach.

It was ugly. And a dark sultry anger towards the village men, who kept shining their flashlight as they brusquely examined him, started to swell inside us. If they had gone on with their disrespectful physical examination, some of us would have yelled and leapt at them. But they got up suddenly and went out into the garden, leaving the body behind.

A late moon had just risen. Through the narrow gap in the wooden door, which had been left open, we saw a number of dark clusters of villagers speaking in low voices and facing the headman and the blacksmith. Perhaps because of their excitement, their discussions were conducted in a grunting dialect incomprehensible to us, and we could only gaze at them as if they were a pack of dogs jostling and barking.

The headman shouted in a harsh tone as though giving orders, and a long silence followed. Once more the headman shouted, then the gathering of villagers broke up and they started to cross the garden. When the blacksmith jumped up on the verandah and began to close the wooden door, I tried to question him. Black and brawny with the moon shining at his back, he shut the door, showing no inclination to indulge me. But he left hastily without locking it. Huddled in the corner as far as possible from the body, hugging our knees, we heard the village adults' footsteps recede and, inside ourselves, felt our own excitement subside and die away like a sound. Now we did not know why we had shouted and banged on the wooden door. There was nothing children could do about the dead.

My brother showed his face, filthy with grease and ash and iron grey in the light from a knothole in the door. He looked towards me, his brown eyes gleaming like currants, the traces of tears and fright still remaining.

'Eh?' I said.

He ran his tongue round his lips, which immediately recovered their vivid colour and resilience.

'I'm cold.'

'What is it, aren't you wearing your coat?' I said, touching his trembling shoulders.

'I lent it to that boy, because he was freezing,' he said, twisting his head towards the body.

'During the day?'

'Yeah.'

'There's no point letting him wear it now,' I said to him angrily. 'Get it back.'

'Ah,' he said vaguely, lowering his eyes.

'I'll get it for you,' I said and stood up. And he followed me promptly, as if afraid to be left behind.

To get my brother's green coat, I had to push and move the dead boy's heavy body quite roughly. As I pulled the coat off the dead boy, who swayed unsteadily and turned over, I felt my comrades' eyes in the darkness all over me. But there was nothing else I could do.

The coat smelt of fruit rapidly broken down by chemicals, not by the long action of bacteria; it smelt of inorganic decay. My brother did not thrust his arms into the coat but hung it over his shoulders and, bending down, gazed at the face of the dead boy, which floated up a ghostly white. Then quiet sobbing shook his body.

'He was my friend, he was my friend,' he repeated, choking with sobs.

Behind him, I saw the small birdlike face of our comrade who had spent the long journey with us, upturned and stiff, and in it his cold, dark, wide-open eyes. Tears ran down my cheeks and dropped onto my brother's shoulder.

Hugging him, I made him stand up and we went back to the corner, forsaking our comrade who had changed into a corpse once again with his eyes still open. Even after we had sat down among our assembled company, my brother went on shaking with little sobs, and that brought back my own and my comrades' grief and made it worse.

We were silent and still for a long time. Then the alarm bell rang out. We were worried and pricked up our ears, but the bell soon stopped, and not long after that an extraordinary commotion arose from the bottom of the slope, around the paved village road. It seemed to spread out from there like ripples to every part of the village. People's footsteps, bumping noises like furniture being moved and horses' sudden neighing. Then dogs' incessant barking and infants' stifled screams.

By and by the sound gathered at the bottom of the slope and seemed to begin to move slowly. I searched for Minami's face in the darkness and found him looking for me. We stared into each other's eyes, almost close enough to touch foreheads.

'Hey,' Minami said in a low voice.

'Let's go and see.' I said.

We jumped up and pressed our shoulders as hard as we could against the wooden door which the blacksmith had forgotten to lock. It opened noisily, and Minami and I jumped down barefoot into the cold garden, followed by my brother. Minami shouted in a biting voice at our comrades who were hurriedly getting up.

'You, stay inside, keep a watch over the dead body. Wild dogs'll come and eat him.'

'Stay and wait,' I also shouted. 'I'll punish anyone who comes out.'

My comrades showed their displeasure, but didn't try to come out. Minami, my brother and I ran down the path through the garden.

When we came to the corner that overlooked the wide road through the gap in the low stone wall, running on pebbles that were cold under our bare soles, the heavily suppressed yet rising clamour and footsteps came blowing toward us on the mist-bearing night wind. Then we suddenly saw a crowd moving along the road and could hardly breathe for shock.

In the dark bluish-grey moonlight, shadowy figures were slowly walking along, bent over and burdened with the heavy luggage on their backs. Children, women, old people, as well as the grown men, were carrying packages on their backs and holding bundles in their hands. Then the sound of carts crunching stones, and goats and cattle pulled along by women. The moonlight tinged the stiff white hair on the goats' crested backs with its wet gloss and had the same effect on the children's heads.

They were going up the road in a body, with two men holding guns following behind — probably for protection, but it looked as if they were herding the villagers to an unknown destination, like driving cattle to the slaughterhouse. The villagers plodded on in complete silence, bent over. And after their exodus, the road and small houses along it looked terribly empty in the moonlight.

'Ah,' my brother sighed weakly, as if almost fainting from extreme astonishment.

'Ah,' Minami groaned. 'Them.'

'Even the goats,' said my brother. 'They're even taking the cattle.'

'They're running away,' Minami said angrily, suddenly realizing. 'At this time of night, they're running away.'

'Yeah,' I said, 'They're running away.'

We fell silent and jumped off the stone wall, crossed a narrow field, and ran towards the road. The cold late-night air, heavy with mist, stung our cheeks and eyelids like a hard powder, but our blood seethed as if with intoxication, and we were wild. On the road, grain scattered by the line of fleeing villagers faintly reflected the moonlight. Already the line was no longer in sight. Hurrying with muffled footsteps, we hid in the lower branches of an old apricot tree and watched the villagers as they walked away up the crest of the curved road. When they disappeared again, we moved to a place where we could see the rearguard, running like small animals.

'They're running away,' my brother said, imitating Minami's tone. His voice was hoarse as if mad with rage, but strangely weak. 'They're even taking the goats.'

'They're running away,' Minami said as well. 'Why?'

I and Minami, who was spraying saliva from his pouting lips and whose eyes were round like an infant's, gazed at each other.

'I don't know, I haven't got the faintest idea,' I lied cautiously.

Minami growled and bit his nails in irritation. A child's screams rose up from the crowd of villagers moving on far above, apparently curbed by an adult hand over his small mouth. A dog howled sadly, and my brother's shoulders twitched.

'Shall we run away too and join them?' said Minami.

'The warden'll be coming to this village leading the next party,' I said.

'I don't care; the villagers have run away, let's go and join them.'

But Minami and I knew that if the villagers had had any intention of taking us along they wouldn't have shut us up inside the dark temple. We knew that they were running away stealthily in the moonlight with no intention of taking us along. So I went on tailing them, hidden in the shadows on either side of the road, instead of returning to call our comrades. What else could I do?

Suddenly we heard hurried footsteps coming down the road, and as soon as we had taken shelter in a sparse thicket of shrubs coated with mist droplets, the blacksmith ran past in the moonlight right before our eyes. He was running down the hill with his body twisted, holding the stock of the rifle slung on his back with his arm against his hip to keep it from bouncing. Hope made our skin glow all over. The main body of the villagers seemed to be waiting where the road entered the forest. Ah, there's still time, I thought. We'll be saved from abandonment in a valley where a terrible plague is raging.

But my expectation collapsed, disappointed. Almost at once the blacksmith came running back carrying a bulky basket in his right arm. He was panting freezing breath, clearly visible even in the dark. Then we were aghast to see a white rabbit jumping in panic inside his basket. There was the din of the villagers starting to move again, but we sat down and didn't move. Our bare feet had gone completely numb and seemed all swollen up. And cold surged up and spread through our flushed bodies. Minami turned back to me. I watched his face, which was a strange mixture of delicate morbid crudity and childishness, like a young beast. It twitched all over, and his mouth opened unable to make a sound. In an instant, tears came oozing out of his eyes.

'I. . .' he said, a feverish voice barely leaking from his throat. 'I'll let everyone know. I'll let them know how we've been abandoned.'

Then he ran out of the thicket, making a ludicrous, obscene gesture. Hugging my brother's shoulders, I rose slowly and came out of hiding. We stood completely exposed in the moonlight, but already the villagers were out of sight along the road going into the forest and we could only occasionally hear a dog barking beyond it. Then the slapping noise of Minami running down the road at full speed.

We went aimlessly up to the edge of the forest and sat down on a low bank. The moon was almost hidden by the forest trees, and it was daybreak that lit up the thick grey sky from behind with a pearly lustre. It was terribly cold. The mist which had begun to thicken limited visibility. My brother and I didn't know what to do. Even if we ran back and stirred up our comrades, it would be no use. Furthermore, I was so tired that it was too much trouble to even walk another step.

'Sleep for a bit,' I said in a voice moist with tears.

'My coat smells,' my brother said, pressing his forehead against my side and curling up against me. 'I don't want to wear this coat.'

'When the sun comes up, let's wash it in the river,' I said, encouraging him, though I wondered if we could wash anything in that tiny narrow river.

'Yeah,' he said, wriggling as he pressed his body against me. 'Let's wash it.'

'It'll soon dry once the wind starts blowing,' I said, and I put my hand on his back and gently rocked him. 'A south wind's best.'

'In the morning, it'll soon dry,' he said weakly in a voice already dissolving into sleep, then he gave a little yawn, and already he had fallen fast asleep in that uncomfortable position.

I was left exhausted and defeated, and completely alone. I took my hand off my brother, hugged my knees and lowered my head. The coat covering him certainly had kept the corpse's smell; a vague, floating impression. I thought as hard as I could about washing the coat in the river when dawn came and drying it in a south wind. I needed to think of something as hard as I could. I didn't want to think about being abandoned.

Chapter Four:
Closure

At dawn the village was deathly still; no cocks crowed and no domestic animals bayed. Morning sun soft and white as powder bathed the inert, debilitated houses, the trees, the lanes and the deep hollow of the valley enfolding them all. It bathed the village like clear water and cast no shadows at the feet of us abandoned boys as we walked slowly along the road, going up and down the slope.

Whatever happened, we couldn't stay inside the dark temple, as we wanted to get away from the corpse of our comrade which gave off a damp smell as it lay there silently like a tree or like a house. So we walked slowly down the village road which was as bleak and deserted as a dune beside a rough sea, our eyes puffy with sleeplessness, leaning forward, putting our hands in our coat pockets.

We were weighed down with anxiety, but we walked silently in twos and threes, keeping each other company on the frost-covered village road and, when we bumped into other comrades coming down with disgruntled expressions, we exchanged silent smiles and signalled to each other by whistling, moved by a strange sense of bubbling incongruity. We were a little overwhelmed by the village entirely without its villagers, the hollow cast-off husk of the village, and grew uneasy about the situation we had fallen into, like the times when we had performed at school functions. The violent excitement of when we learned of the villagers' exodus and the first hour afterwards was already diluted, and we felt as if our show of silent respect towards the strange state of the empty village would make us burst out laughing unless we clenched our back teeth. And without a supervisor there was nothing for us to do. We didn't know what to do. So, slowly and doggedly, we walked up and down the road.

The village was quiet, and the sky covering the valley had cleared to a touching vivid pale blue. The mountainside with the abandoned mine directly across the valley looked as though many small fish were swimming furiously when the leaves of the shrubs showed their silvery-grey undersides as the wind blew. Then, after a short while, the sea of foliage over the road we were walking on stirred, showing that the wind had veered. But the wind didn't come down to the level of our heads and shoulders, and the sun was warm. Each house was locked with a stout iron padlock or bolts entwined with chains and was silent. We walked slowly between the houses.

When the sun cleared the mountain ridge, it was noon. Walking along the road, we heard the wall clocks in the sealed and deserted houses telling the hour. Then, without warning, hunger threatened us. Holding our breath and a little scared, we fetched our kit-bags, which had hard tack in them, from the room where our dead comrade lay stinking, and went back to the square in front of the school, where we ate. The only reason everyone gathered there was that there was a small hand-pump which produced a trickle of cloudy water when pumped with all one's strength. That was no special reason. The reason for keep-ing this strange, droll silence, heavy with unnatural awkwardness, was unclear as well. We were probably the only ones left in the silent village, and we all had a common feeling of being crushed by the same surprise. Since we shared the same state and the same feeling, what dissension could there be?

But when the meal was over, our full stomachs brought an irritating fatigue and sorrow to some, and caused a foolish satisfaction in others. So we began wagging our tongues in contrary ways.

'Why did they run away?' one of my comrades asked me. 'Do you know?'

'Why did they?' asked my brother, who was sitting next to me hugging his knees, his head on one side.

'I don't know,' I said.

Once more a languid silence spread over the village and the valley, drawing a ring around us, and the echoes reverberated. We lay down on the flagstones or leaned against tree trunks and gazed up absent-mindedly at the sky, which soaked through strangely to the backs of our heads.

'You, hey, you,' Minami said, getting up suddenly and looking at me. 'You didn't drink the water from this well, did you?'

'Uh?' I said, bemused.

'Why not?' Minami earnestly plied me with questions. 'I know it's because you're scared of the plague. The village folk ran away terrified of the plague, abandoning us in the middle of swarms of germs.'

The agitation caught everyone. I thought I must restore their balance. Otherwise they would become desperate and start getting violent. It was a pressing problem for me as well.

'Plague?' I said, twisting my lips as if deriding Minami. 'I never thought of anything like that.'

'What about the village woman who died in the warehouse? And our mate,' he said .

'He was ill before we came here,' I said. 'Wasn't he, everyone?'

'There were the animals too,' Minami said, after thinking a bit. 'Such a lot of animals died.'

The memory of the sight and smell of those piled-up animal carcasses, which we had buried only yesterday, rose up immediately and disturbed me. What really was the cause. . . ?

'Rat's disease, rutting rabbit's disease,' I said, rubbing in my derision. 'Anyone who's scared of that, run away with the villagers!'

'I'm going to run for it,' said Minami, slinging his kit-bag on his shoulder and getting up vigorously, showing his determination. 'I don't want to die. You can stay here, groaning with the plague, and wait for the warden to bring the next party.'

One by one, our comrades got up and followed him, until my brother and I were the only ones left. We looked each other in the eye. The smooth skin round my brother's mouth was trembling with anxiety. When Minami and the others started to walk up the paved road we followed, showing our disagreement by deliberately leaving our kit-bags behind.

My brother and I climbed the zig-zagging road up the slope and on to the forest road piled high with damp, dead leaves, keeping a little distance between ourselves and Minami's group, our arms round each other's shoulders. We tried to flaunt our fraternal bond in opposition to the others, but I wasn't sure that we could remain in the village after they had left. So when my brother squeezed my side with his encircling arm and gazed up at me with feverish eyes, I cruelly ignored him. His eyes were asking: I wonder if it's really the plague; the shrews and the rest died as well? Then I repeated to myself: I don't know, how should I know such a thing?

Coming out of the forest, Minami and the others stopped dumbfounded at the head of the trolley track, and my brother and I, forgetting ourselves, ran up to them. The small split between us had already vanished and we gazed at the other end of the track as a single group, as a group of the dumbfounded. After that we sighed bitterly.

On the section of the trolley track across the valley closest to the mountainside opposite, a kind of malevolent barricade had been built out of tree stumps, boards, railway sleepers and rocks, cutting us off. To try to climb over that piled-up barricade on the narrow track would inevitably mean falling to the valley bottom, feet entangled by collapsing rocks and pieces of wood. That barricade stood in our way like a strong wall; moreover, it was there as a trap full of dangerous instability. And in the deep valley bottom raged the fierce sound of water left over from the persistent flooding in the upper reaches.

What stopped us at first was the perplexity and short interruption of judgement due to dumbfounded surprise. Though I hadn't thought of crossing the valley and leaving, I was drawn into their mood and choked up, and was just silent.

Presently we saw, through the winter-blasted branches of tall trees, a man appear from the trolley shed on the far side. At first Minami shouted, and after that we all raised our voices and yelled.

'Hey! Hey!' we called, waving our arms and bits of sticks to draw the attention of the man on the far side. Our voices, resounding over each other and echoing in the valley, were like a melancholy chorus.

'Hey! Hey! We're still here! Hey!'

The small brown face on the far side had obviously noticed us. Then he brought a hunting rifle from his shoulder to his chest and moved quickly to the rise on the left of the shed. We let our arms drop and gave up calling from our aching throats. We understood. The man had moved to a vantage point to watch for those bold desperate spirits who might walk out along the track towards the other side. The barricade was built to thwart us, and moreover, there was even a sentinel standing guard. We were cut off.

Sudden anger made us burn. We yelled jeers across to the other side of the valley. But our catcalls dropped into the valley and melted into the sound of the river in its bottom before they could reach the man kneeling on the slope that was covered with bare oak trees and aiming his gun towards the track. We were full of rage, and lonely.

'That bunch do disgusting things,' said Minami, in a

voice shrill with anger. 'They're going to pick off anyone trying to cross the bridge. Disgusting, isn't it?'

'Why? Why will they shoot?' asked my brother, his eyes full of tears. His voice was quavering childishly. 'Pick us off. . .?'

'We aren't even their enemies,' said another of the group tearfully, prompted by my brother's agitation. 'We're not their enemies.'

'To cut us off,' Minami shouted. 'Stop whining. They want to cut us off. Understand?'

'Why cut us off?' my brother said weakly, overawed by the violence in Minami's voice.

'You, me, we've all caught the plague,' said Minami. 'They were afraid of us scattering germs everywhere. So they cut us off to watch us dying like dogs or shrews.'

'But we haven't got the plague,' I said by way of informing the other comrades, glaring at Minami. 'They just think we have. Has anyone vomited since this morning? Has anyone had red spots break out all over their body? Or been infested with lice?'

They were all silent. I bit my lip hard during the brief echo of my voice.

'Let's go back,' said Minami after a short time. 'I'd rather catch the plague than be shot.'

Then he kicked the behind of the boy in front of him with a strange yelp and started to run. I followed him and ran down the road which went through the forest. I ran haphazardly, out of breath, following Minami who was running flat out, and caught up with him as he stopped exhausted at the edge of the forest. For a while he and I just panted, unable to make a sound. Our younger comrades, trailing far behind us, came running after, making the forest resound, like a sudden gust of wind which was the harbinger of a storm. The noise seemed to be prompted by anxiety, like a scream.

'You, don't ever mention the plague again,' I said to Minami in a hoarse voice. 'If they start bawling because of you, I'll make you regret it.'

Rallying against my threats, he jerked his chin up, but he did not actually resist. He only kept silent and showed an unsettled, irritated face.

'All right?' I said. 'I won't mention it either,'

'Yeah,' he said in a vague tone. He seemed to be pondering something else. Then he suddenly started blustering.

'If we want to run away, it's easy; even if they're guarding the trolley track, we're not in a hole.'

But I knew very well that he was bluffing. I kept silent, feeling his irritated gaze on my face. The testimony of the villagers who had hunted the escaped army cadet, the depth of the valley and the force of the current which we had seen with our own eyes, could only convince me of the impossibility of escape.

'We can soon climb the other side of the mountain,' Minami said, countering my mute denial, though his voice had already lost its overbearing force.

'You'll get half killed by the villagers on the other side of the mountain,' I said. 'Just like they did to you when you escaped before.'

The blocking of the trolley track was a 'symbol'. It showed the concentrated hostility of the farmers in the numerous villages surrounding the valley hamlet where we were sealed up, that thick obstinate wall which we could never penetrate. It was clearly impossible for us to con-front it and force our way through it.

'Half killed,' said Minami, groaning. 'I escaped three times and was half killed three times. Only this time there's a man on guard with a hunting rifle. I once helped slaughter sick dogs and cattle. See? Calves groaning from disease; with a hammer as big as their heads.'

'Stop it, if you don't want me to hit you,' I shouted in a frenzy. 'Don't say anything like that again.'

'You'll soon understand,' he said, alert for my attack. 'To hit a sick calf properly, three men would stand it up. I was supposed to distract it with water or grass.'

I was about to jump at his throat. But in a moment his eyes filled with tears. I stopped still, breathing hard.

'You see?' he said, wiping away his tears with the back of his hand. 'I really did it.'

'That's different from us being cut off. None of us are ill,' I said.

'I can't say it right,' he said fretfully. 'I remembered the time when I killed the calves. I remembered it all at once.'

I was almost drawn into the sorrowful exasperation which had descended on him. I could no longer hide the trembling of my lips, caused not only by anger.

'But there's nothing we can do, is there?' I said. 'Don't whine. We're cut off. There's nothing we can do.'

Our comrades, my brother included, caught up with us. Surrounded by them, Minami and I gazed into each other's eyes like the best of friends.

I don't intend to justify what we started late that afternoon. None of us either decided on or passed judgement on it. Although abnormal, it began quite naturally; like that stage of adolescence when children's thighs suddenly grow longer.

What we did first was to choose a house each, or one between two, and violently force open the closed doors. Without experiencing the palpitations and excitement of theft, we discovered the hidden food.

My brother and I chose a house with a cross-striped wall right at one end of the paved road to the valley. When I pulled the padlock out of the door and smashed the bolt with the stone my brother had brought, he rushed, wary but smart as a nimble fish, into the dark interior.

It was dark in there, like a part of the forest abandoned by people. Only the smell of people lingered inside, already decaying, without the lovely freshness of 'life'. There were no strangers' eyes set in the roughcast walls, exposed black beams, or heavy lopsided furniture digging into the tatami spread over the floor, to keep watch on us from the inner recesses when we sneaked into the strangers' house. There were no strangers there, and even more, there were no people there. It was forsaken by people.

My brother and I, treading carelessly on underwear that had been left behind in the rush, strewn over the tatami and on the floorboards, uncovered hidden sacks of rice, a little dried fish and a drop of soy sauce left in the bottom of a cracked old bottle, and carried them out onto the road as if we were picking wayside flowers. We worked slowly and silently. As I threw a tin of ground soybean meal onto the pile of food on the flagstones, having gone in and out several times, Minami called me, twisting his face, as he tried to haul a bag full of some kind of food out of a small thatched house on the corner.

'I've never done such petty thieving,' he said, crestfallen.

'How's your thing now?' I shouted back at him, as he was usually proud of the tremendous erection he got whenever he committed a crime.

'Limp as a girl's rag doll.'

His voice soon vanished, leaving the echoes of an empty feeling, and I went back to my 'petty thieving'. We persisted in it because we had nothing else to do. But that guilty, slipshod labour did not hold enough conviction to keep going. The houses were small, and the goods were shoddy. And they didn't arouse our curiosity even for a moment. My brother and I decided to carry as much as we could manage of our share to the square in front of the school. In the square, our comrades had already piled up their spoils. They were all miserable, shabby sacks of food. They would ensure a fairly long subsistence, but that was all. The boys were exhausted and seemed rather ashamed of the piecemeal harvest before them. We passed comment on the finds, then went back down the slope to fetch the rest of our pickings.

'Hey,' my brother gave a short stifled yelp. 'Over there.'

My slack muscles suddenly tensed all over, and the blood flowed back to my head. In front of the remaining pile of goods stood a Korean boy gazing at us, holding a sack of rice on his shoulder. The silence around the valley, my comrades' sudden dull cries and the late afternoon sunshine enveloped me, and I advanced slowly, glaring at my adversary, my skin blushing all over. The rice sack dropped from his shoulder, and as he lowered his head and crouched, I sprang at him.

The first violent bout without a breathing space: nails digging into each other's flesh, colliding bodies, entangled legs. We fell on the paving stones and rolled around without a sound, kicking and scissoring with our elbows. We fought in silence, with all our strength. The Korean boy's body had a strong smell and was incredibly heavy. I was pinned down by his bulk, my right arm caught by his elbow, and I was unable to move. Fat fingers were thrust into my nostrils and blood started running along my jaw, and I couldn't get my head out from under my adversary's chest. But while he did that he couldn't move his body either, and he was breathing heavily. I stuck out my left arm, extended my fingers and scratched at the ground. I heard my brother's approaching footsteps and the Korean boy's threatening groans; then a hard lump of stone was thrust into my hand by my brother. I struck my adversary on the nape of his neck with a fist made big and heavy by the stone.

The Korean boy groaned, sagged, and slid off my body. Covering my nostrils with my hand, I stood up. Lying there, my enemy, with his round plump childish face, thick fleshy lips and narrow gentle eyes, looked up at me. I lowered my foot, which was poised to kick his defenceless solar plexus as hard as possible, and turned to my brother. He retreated under the roadside trees, hands on his hips, opened his tear-filled eyes wide and stared at us.

I beckoned him over, jerking my chin, and picked up our belongings. Last of all, I stopped him picking up the sack of rice which the Korean boy had tried to snatch. I no longer intended to take it along. Then we went back up the slope, leaving the enemy lying there watching our movements.

'You're strong, Brother,' my brother said in a high voice, his face covered with tears.

'He's strong too,' I said and turned back, dripping blood

from my nose over the goods I was carrying. The Korean boy, limping and carrying the sack, was about to cross the short, narrow unpaved bridge across the valley. He must have been on his way home to the Korean settlement on the hillside opposite. It wasn't only us who got left behind, I thought, a vague feeling swelling up inside me. But the blood went on streaming from my nose, so that it seemed my chest, my hands and the food would all get bloody unless I tilted my head back. My brother, unable to wait, left me behind as I walked slowly on and went running up the paved road to tell the others about my fight with the Korean boy who had suddenly appeared.

The realization that other people besides us had stayed behind disturbed my comrades. But in the evening we found another abandoned 'neighbour'.

What we were doing at that point was choosing our lodgings and cooking supper. We took possession of the houses, each to his taste. My brother and I selected a storehouse-like building at the top of the slope above the school square, probably a granary at harvest time, with an earthen foyer, where empty straw bags and grains of maize lay strewn about, and a low boarded floor which would serve as our place to settle, and carried in the food we had acquired as well as an old flower-patterned blanket. While I brought in firewood and piled it on the earth floor, my brother picked vegetables from the small field behind the storehouse and hunted out a pot in a farmhouse nearby. We put pieces of shredded vegetable, dried fish and some handfuls of rice into the pot, and went to pump water into it in front of the school.

Our comrades were milling about in front of the warehouse and peering into its interior through the open door. The evening sun made grape-coloured shadows on their immature but sturdy bodies, pressed close together and piled upon each other. They were all overwhelmed by amazement. My brother and I ran up and saw, inside the dark warehouse, a dead body lying covered with a cloth and, sitting next to it, a girl, detached yet full of hostility. I gazed at her with my comrades, panting. I couldn't suppress an astonished sigh.

'She was left behind,' Minami said excitedly in a low, feverish voice, pushing aside the crowd of boys and coming up to me, 'In the middle of the funeral, because everyone ran away. They do disgusting things.'

'Ah,' I said, and gazed at the girl's small, motionless head with its frightened eyes turned towards us and, visible beneath her lightly poised hand, the supine corpse's forehead, like a plant. The outside air, tinged with evening's golden lustre, had just begun to steal in.

'Have a good smell, it stinks,' Minami sniffed. 'The same smell as a dead dog.'

'Who found them?'

'Someone thought of sleeping in here,' he said, with an excited giggle. 'A dead woman and a mad girl. Someone wanted to sleep with them.'

'Now, everybody, stop looking,' I said, revolted by the sight of the girl's mouth, half-open with fear, pink gums and tensed twitching cheeks, all of which were filthy and hardly beautiful. And I didn't want to see the dead body.

'Whoever opened the door, shut it,' said Minami.

As one of our comrades went fearfully up to the door,

the girl's face twitched like an advance warning of tears. Then, when the door was about to close, sobbing came from behind it. The girl immediately became a mystery and grew and expanded. The door got stuck awkwardly and didn't close properly, but the boy detailed to shut it stopped his work halfway, his back trembling, clearly overcome by fear. So we stood still for a little while. But it was creepy. Then, each with a heavy load on his mind, we returned to our lodgings and went on with the business of cooking supper.

Lighting a fire in the piled-up wood on the earth floor, we placed the pot on the small flame and, waiting while we endured incredible hunger, we discussed our bothersome new neighbour.

'That girl,' my brother said thoughtfully, 'she must have gone mad because her mother died.'

'How do you know she's mad?'

'That dirty girl,' he said vaguely, 'isn't she?'

'Yeah,' I said, groaning. 'She was a bit dirty.'

The rice porridge cooked so fast we could hardly believe it, and the taste wasn't bad either. We eagerly ate our feast in silence, using the mess kits from our bags. The flames in the pile of firewood in the middle of the earthen floor warmed the air inside the storehouse and a mysterious damp smell came flooding out. Completely full, our bodies flabby with warmth like molluscs, we lay down on the straw spread over the floorboards, wrapped in the blanket. It was night: we were at liberty in the village. We had to will ourselves to sleep. My brother closed his eyes, pulling the rough blanket which smelt of sweat and grease up to his chin, and breathed softly. I thought I might take the remainder of the porridge to the girl in the warehouse. But it was too much trouble. Besides, I was scared of the woman's bloated body lying next to her. The image of the corpse I had seen in the dim evening light started to rise up before me. Also our dead comrade, lying face up in the now-deserted temple building. I thought about death and was gripped by feelings which choked my chest and made my throat dry, a sudden pushing and shoving in my guts. It was a sort of chronic ailment I had. Once that feeling and that agitation of my whole body had begun, I wouldn't be able to shake it off until I got to sleep. And I couldn't recall it with the same impact in daytime. My back and thighs were soaked in sweat and, submerged in it, I sank up to my head. 'Death', for me, was my non-existence in a hundred years' time and, in a few hundred years' time, my non-existence in a boundless far future. Even in that distant future wars would break out, children would be sent to reformatories, some would prostitute themselves with homosexuals and some would have fairly healthy sex lives. But then I wouldn't be there. Biting my lips, seething with anger, my chest constricted by anxiety, I pondered. By now, countless germs must be spurting out of the two corpses making the air in the narrow valley glutinous. What was worse, there was nothing we could do. I shivered in horror.

'Eh?' my brother said.

'It's nothing,' I said hoarsely. 'Go to sleep, quick.'

'Aren't you cold?' he said bashfully after being silent for a while. 'A draught's coming in.'

I got up abruptly and went to cover up the cracks in the wooden front door, peeling one of the straw mats from the floor. Through a chink, I saw a gentle blaze of burning firewood somewhere around the Korean settlement on the mountainside opposite, flickering like a signal. He's lit a fire, I thought, feeling a small hot sensation like friendship deep in my body, like a bud. The light bruising all over me and the pain in my nostrils came back to me like a small pleasure. He was really strong; some Koreans are very strong, so when we fight, it takes time.

'Show me your camel tin-opener,' my brother said in a wheedling voice. 'Go on, just for a bit.'

I took a tin-opener in the shape of a camel's head from my kit-bag and placed it in his outstretched hand. It was useless right now, but my brother and I liked it best of all, and he wanted me to give it to him. When I got under the blanket once again, he pressed his back, his warm, familiar back, against me.

'Hey,' I said gently. 'You're not scared?'

'Uh?' he said sleepily after giving a weak yawn. 'This camel tin-opener, would you lend me it for a while? Can I keep it in my bag?'

'Give it back later,' I said magnanimously.

The fire on the earth floor was almost out, and the cries of animals in the forest surrounding the valley, birds' sudden wingbeats and sounds of tree bark splitting in the cold echoed around. Overwhelmed by the provocative, hopeless, oppressive image of death, making a painful effort to get to sleep, I was so jealous when I heard my brother's peaceful breathing that I could have lost my tender feelings towards him. Inside the village, the abandoned and the unburied dead were either sleeping or suffering from sleeplessness; outside the village, all the malicious folk were fast asleep.

Chapter Five:
Solidarity of the Abandoned

Next morning my brother and I cooked porridge again in virtual silence and finished it as we sat facing the fire on the earth floor. Neither of us had any appetite. The village was absolutely still.

Outside, the weak soft winter sunshine was all-enveloping. The frost pillars on both sides of the road were crumbling. We pulled our coat collars up around our necks and went down the slope. Our comrades were squatting or walking round aimlessly in the square in front of the school. The lazy air, the apathy which had seized them, came to attack me like a poison.

We sat down on a stone in a corner of the square and hugged our knees. The group round Minami started playing leapfrog, but as they went on doing it reluctantly and with scant interest, the onlookers grew irritated. Even though it involved vigorous movement, it was no more interesting than sitting down hugging one's knees after all. Bored with leapfrog, Minami and the others formed a circle, slid their trousers down and let the wind blow on their bellies. Obscene giggles and raucous jeers. Their penises, bathed in the bright sunshine, slowly grew erect, slowly grew limp, then grew erect again. The autonomous motion of their genitals, without the rude vigour of desire or the calm of fulfilment, went on for a long time under everyone's eyes. And it wasn't interesting either.

During that spiritless play, we peered at an antique wall clock which one of our comrades had brought out or, looking up at the sky, tried to calculate the time by the sun's position. But time went really slowly and simply wouldn't pass. Time doesn't move at all, I thought in irritation. Like a domestic animal, time doesn't move without human beings' strict supervision. Like a horse or a sheep, time won't move a step without grown-ups' orders. We are a steady state in the stagnation of time. There's nothing to do. But there is nothing harder, more irritating and more poisonously fatiguing in the depths of your body than being shut up doing nothing. I got up shivering.

'Eh?' my brother said, looking up with vague, unfocused eyes.

'I'm going to give the rest of the porridge to the girl in the warehouse,' I said, suddenly hitting on the idea.

'Fine,' he said weakly, bowing his head and showing the nape of his neck, which was thin and dirty yet revealed a heartrending beauty. 'I'll go and look for some tasty vegetables.'

'It'd be good if you could find some Chinese cabbage,' I said and ran up the slope to the granary, leaving him behind.

The porridge had congealed and gone cold in the bottom of the cooking pot. Seeing it, I hesitated, but didn't abandon my plan. I had nothing else to do. And for us, cut off in the village, everything was just as cold and set, and refused to melt softly. Running back, I thought how very far from softness and warmth the road, the leafless trees, the school building and my squatting comrades, slumped like beasts, really were.

The heavy warehouse door was closed, leaving a narrow chink. I peeped in and was disturbed to see the girl's face right there, illuminated by the white, unnaturally powdery light. She was looking steadily at me, eyes swollen from lack of sleep. And behind her narrow shoulders, the corpse was still staring upwards. She had moved away from it because of the smell, and was trying to inhale fresh air through the chink, I thought, feeling new disgust breaking out. I quickly thrust the pot through the chink.

The girl suddenly stood up, scared. My flustered voice was strangely hoarse and timid.

'Hey, you, eat this; hey.'

She bowed silently, nervous as a bird. I spoke again, angry at the slow stupid tone of my voice.

'Your mother's dead, isn't she? Come on, eat.'

She covered her ears and kept obstinately silent. I turned round violently and ran up the road, biting my lips in anger. The fool, the fool, I muttered hoarsely to myself, cursing the girl, but somehow if I had stopped my screed of abuse I would have cried. Something must have come over me.

When I got back to the square, my comrades had gathered together, and in the midst of them was my brother, bending over with a feverish expression and holding between his knees, instead of a Chinese cabbage, a shabby, rather unhealthy-looking medium-sized dog. The dog was rubbing its nose familiarly against his chest and howling as if from starvation.

'Hey, that creature, where did you find it?' I asked, breathless with surprise. 'That dog, where was it?'

He stammered in reply, showing uncontrollable pride and joy and perplexity all over his copper-shadowed face.

'He can't speak because he's so pleased at finding the dog,' Minami interrupted in a disgruntled voice of mingled envy and scorn. 'Let's beat it to death and eat it.'

My brother jerked his shoulders and hugged the dog. Looking up, he glared at Minami in a fierce manner brimming over with tension.

'Look, look,' Minami said, offended by my brother's sullenness, emphasizing his scorn. 'He's clinging to the dog and won't let go. He's making his tiny finger-sized dog-diddling thing hard.'

My brother endured the boys' tumultuous laughter, biting his lips and trembling with rage.

'Take it and give it some dried fish,' I said assertively, restraining Minami and the others. 'Pay no attention to them.'

The younger boys followed my brother, who had recovered his composure and was leading the dog to the granary, whistling to it in short bursts. Minami stared at me with eyes that held a crafty half-smile, then kicked a stone with the tip of his shoe. Since he and I were both bored, it would have been good if only something were to happen, but we didn't have the energy to fight each other.

We were galled by the stubborn procrastination of time and the silence blanketing the valley, and we began to grow tired. And we were expecting something. Anything which restored our integrity and tension would have been welcome, even the return of the villagers. We had broken into and robbed their houses and occupied their living quarters, but already we no longer knew whether or not we hated those who had abandoned us.

In the early afternoon, I went to the warehouse to fetch back the pot to cook porridge for lunch, a prospect which hardly whetted my appetite at all. The cooking pot, completely empty, had been pushed just outside the door. I peered inside and stared for a short while into the girl's weak eyes, which were gradually growing less wary. But we didn't talk to each other. After the meal, I divided the leftovers, gave one half to the dog, which was rubbing its head against my brother's hip without trying to leave, and took the other half to the girl. She stared from the darkness behind the door at the pot I held out. But she wouldn't reach out and take it. I put it down on the floor and, since I felt that she must want water, I went to the pump in front of the school to fill the old flask.

When I came back, the girl was eagerly chewing the food from the pot. I pointed out the flask to her, though she was still exhibiting a set countenance, and went back quite satisfied. As for my brother's dog, it was frantically wolfing down not just our porridge but all sorts of things laid out for it by our comrades.

Late in the afternoon, after thickly clotted time had passed, we saw a boy carrying a bulky bundle wrapped in a white cloth on his back slowly come down the narrow path from the Korean settlement to the valley, which cut diagonally across the middle of the mountainside opposite. We realized immediately that it was my opponent in the fight and that the object he carried on his back, though cloth-wrapped, was obviously the body of a dead grown-up. We were transfixed.

We eagerly watched the Korean boy awkwardly tense his strong limbs to support the heavy weight. When his head and the white lump disappeared behind the school building we went down the alley, which was filled with damp, piss-smelling air streaming from the thatched roofs along it, and came out on the grassy slope which led to the valley. Then we slowly made our way down our side of the slope as the Korean boy descended. It was clear that he had noticed us, but he stubbornly looked down and ignored us until he had reached the flat meadow on the valley floor, right beside the narrow river, where the fruits of our first labours in the village were buried.

After that, he put the lump down in the meadow, threw our silent group one swift glance from his sharp eyes, then went off up the narrow path at terrific speed and came back down carrying a hoe over his shoulder like a gun. Before he could start digging up the meadow right by the white lump he had laid down, we were galvanized by his intention. As he would bury his dead, so we would bury ours. We questioned each other with feverish glances.

'Hey,' said Minami, 'let's bury him.'

'Let's do it,' I said, gaining strength.

'We'll carry him here,' he said quickly, interrupting me. 'You dig a hole, you and two or three of the others.'

I nodded and ran up to the shed-like building which held the hoes. My brother was squatting at the top of the slope stroking the back of the frightened dog, which had been yelping and twitching its tail ever since the Korean boy appeared.

We started work. I knew that my brother was itching to join in, but when the hole was almost dug and Minami and the others came down carrying our former comrade wrapped in a blanket, the dog let out a dreadful howl as if it was being strangled, writhing and pushing its head between my brother's legs, so I couldn't call him to work.

From our experience of burying the carcasses of dogs, cats, rats and so on, we knew that we would have to dig a hole of considerable width and depth in order to bury a human corpse. So when Minami and the others had laid down the body, tightly wrapped in the blanket, at the top of the meadow behind the slight mound where we had buried the animals, they came to help us dig the hole. On the other side of the valley, the Korean boy, raising the hoe with his arms and shoulders almost vertical, was digging a hole for his dead.

After we had started sweating in our thick underwear, with the dirt trapped inside giving off a musty smell, we carried the thing wrapped in the blanket to the hole and put it in, but the hole was still too shallow. We pulled out the bundle, now soiled with new earth, and once again got into the hole and swung the hoes.

It seemed that the work on the far side of the valley wasn't going well either. Ground water started to ooze up from the bottom of the hole we had dug. We laid the blanket-wrapped corpse in the fast-deepening pool of red-brown water. Leaving Minami and the others, who carefully laid out the corpse as if planting bulbs, then busied themselves covering it with soft earth, I went and sat down beside my brother who was squatting with the dog held against his knees. From the top of the meadow where we huddled together, the hole where we had buried our dead and the hole where we had buried the huge number of animal carcasses looked like the beginning of a regular series, as if they were a pair of reference points. I thought of simple graves laid out endlessly from those reference points at equal intervals, countless bodies to be disposed of. With all the battlefields in the world, how many people are going to die? And how many more people are going to dig the holes to bury them in. It seemed to me that our single grave was going to spread out forever all over the world.

Our friend was now lying in the earth, the ground water soaking into his skin, his hair and the soft tissues of his anus. And the ground water was flowing under the earth's surface after seeping through innumerable beasts' carcasses and would eventually be sucked up by the tough roots of the grass.

I was crushed and didn't want to think about it. I stood up and looked across the river. The Korean boy had also finished his burial. He was struggling to pick up a nearby stone so big that he could hardly get his arms around. I understood his admirable intention. Either he would put the stone up as a monument to the dead or he would place it as a heavy lid for fear of the corpse rising up in the middle of the night. Whichever it was, such conduct was heroic and appealed to my downcast spirit. I ran down the slope and patted Minami, who was piling an earth mound over the grave, on the shoulder.

'Huh?' he said, raising his flushed face.

'Look,' I said and pointed to the other side, though the tall grass and the undulations of the ground hid the Korean boy who was bending over the stone. 'He's in trouble; let's help him.'

Minami stared at me with a puzzled expression. But he followed me as I ran off without another thought. We jumped over the river and ran across the grass on the other side. The Korean boy quickly straightened his big frame, ready to attack, and watched our approach.

'We'll help you,' I shouted, waving my arms 'That stone's heavy, isn't it? We'll give you a hand.'

'You can't carry it by yourself,' said Minami.

The boy looked at us with eyes full of suspicion, then a bemused expression gradually spread from his thick lips. We went up to him, our arms dangling, showing that we had no intention of launching a sneak attack. He blushed, probably from embarrassment and excitement. We helped him to pick up the stone. When it was securely settled on top of the earth mound we sighed contentedly and the three of us straightened up and turned to each other. We were all at a loss because of our sudden idleness, and felt awkward.

'Was it your place that was flying the red paper flag?' Minami asked, embarrassed, in a voice that caught in his throat. 'Did your mother die?'

'My father,' the Korean boy declared, moving his lips slowly. 'My father died. My mother ran away with the villagers.'

'Why didn't you run away?' asked Minami.

'My father died, so I didn't run away,' he said.

'Oh, your father,' said Minami vaguely, then shut his mouth, finally satisfied. The Korean boy turned his dazzling eyes from him to me, then stared at my red and swollen nostrils. I stared back at several blue-black smudges on his broad, flat face. A smile hovered around my adversary's lips.

'What's your name?' I asked in a rush. 'Eh?'

'Li.' The boy lowered his head to hide the irrepressible smile which flitted across his cheeks and wrote his name in the soft sloping surface of the earth mound with the toe of the plaited straw sandal that he wore without socks.

'Oh,' I mumbled deep in my throat, but in fact I was impressed with the beauty of the single character formed by the lines he had drawn. 'Li, is it?'

'I don't mind about the other morning,' Li said, still looking down.

'I don't mind about it at all,' I replied.

We looked each other in the eyes and smiled for no reason. I realized that I'd taken a liking to Li.

'Have you buried him?' he asked Minami nonchalantly, with the intimacy of a fellow human being. 'Somebody's dead, isn't he?'

'One of our mates.'

'There's another one; a woman's died in the warehouse,' I added, suddenly remembering. 'That means three people in the village have died.'

'The evacuee in the warehouse,' Li said, evidently interested, 'have you buried her already?'

'No, we haven't buried her yet,' I said.

'Any plague victim who isn't buried will infect the living,' Minami said authoritatively. 'I heard that from the warden in the reformatory.'

'We can't take her out and bury her,' I said, 'because the girl stayed there with her.'

'I know that girl,' Li shouted, showing his broad white teeth, his eyes shining with pride. 'I'll talk to her.'

'Then we'll bury her,' said Minami, in a high voice matching Li's tone. 'We'll bury anything.'

Flanking Li, we jumped across the stream and went back to our excited comrades.

I took charge of digging a hole a size larger than the one we had dug for our comrade, for the woman's body which Li and the others were going to bring down. Li and Minami, taking half the boys with them, ran up the steep slope, slipping repeatedly on the green grass covered with yellow withered leaves and stems, howling like natives from a savage tribe.

As we were already used to digging holes, the work went well. We slogged on, divided into teams swinging hoes and raking the earth. Insects crawled out from under the surface, and we stamped on them at once. Li and the others must have been talking things over with the girl in front of the corpse in the warehouse, and didn't come back for quite a while. After a long time had passed, we heard loud voices from the road. I left the group to finish off and went up the muddy path, which was just drying off after the quaggy thaw of the frost in the meadow.

Sure enough, Minami and his aides came marching along the road, bearing the dead woman on their shoulders, wrapped in blankets and white sheets, as if carrying a broken-legged calf. The others lent support with outstretched arms. And the tall Li was bending down to talk to the girl, who kept apart from the pack but followed them intently. The pallbearers passed me as I stood beside the flagstones looking on. Then the girl came by, palefaced, with cracked lips and eyes filled with tears. She paid no attention to me, her eyes set straight ahead, her shoulders trembling with suppressed sobs.

'Look, it can't be helped, she's dead,' Li earnestly consoled her. 'Your mother's dead, isn't she? She stinks. We've got to bury her.'

I went straight down after them. My group was silently and diligently digging up the earth. Perhaps because they felt some diffidence towards the girl, and because they had nothing else to do, Minami's party stood holding the corpse in their arms. The girl halted at the top of the meadow, ignoring Li's calls, sat down, and wouldn't go anywhere near the hole. She watched the work with tears running down her cheeks and her shoulders shaking with sobs.

Deft as undertakers, our comrades laid the corpse in the bottom of the hole and covered it with earth. The girl whimpered with her face buried in her knees. Li and I felt uneasy standing by. So we left the crying girl and went down to the scene of operations.

'Shall we put stones on them?' Minami asked Li as he came up. 'I don't know what to do after burials n' things.'

'Pack down the earth,' Li said. 'Stamp on it and pack it down.'

We hesitated. Then we gingerly got up on the soft, not especially tall earth mounds over the doubled-up corpses. We split up into three gangs for the three mounds. My brother, unable to stand aside, went and joined the others who were trampling down the animals' grave.

As we followed Li's example and began slowly stamping down the earth, the mountain ranges all round the valley sank into deep red and only the evening sky over the quiet village remained white. The swiftly falling dusk endowed our labour of foot-stamping with a solemn and definite significance. It was the same as the unbearable image of 'death' which visited me only at night, constricting my chest and bringing the sweat out all over my skin. We went on with our work with renewed fervour.

The primitive Japanese, so terrified of the resurrection of their dead, had folded the legs of the corpses and piled their graves with massively heavy slabs of stone. We too stamped the earth flat with legs strengthened by fear of our friend, once a comrade of ours, rising up from out of the earth and rampaging in the village where children had been left behind alone and cut off.

Then, unexpectedly, we were silently stamping down the earth in a tight ring with our bodies pressed together and our arms entwined, in the fresh air of the thickening night, the cold grainy fog, and the bleak winter wind. We began to forge a firm bond between our bewildered selves. Under the thin surface layer of earth, which retained more of the day's meagre warmth than the fog or our goose-pimpled flesh, they were lying, arms and legs drawn up, their cold dark eyes hidden under dead lids, with squirming maggots already seething in the private places between their thighs.

They scared us, like birds flying up at one's feet, but they were closer to us than the grown-ups toting their hunting rifles on the other side of the valley behind the barricade, the cowardly grown-ups from 'Outside' who thwarted us. Night had fallen, and since there was no one to come running out from the defunct rows of houses calling us with sweet voices, we went on trampling down the earth in silence for a long time, holding on to each others' shoulders.

*

Next morning, when I took out the leftovers from break-fast, the girl was sunning herself on the low stone steps in front of the warehouse. For the first time she took the cooking pot when I held it out to her. That made me glow all over. I thought I would stand and watch while she finished the food. But she didn't start eating for some time.

'At lunch, come and eat at our place,' I said gruffly, and ran off without waiting for a reply.

Lunch came, and the girl still hadn't responded to my invitation. With my brother leading the dog, I took food to her again. She bowed her head low, stroking the dog with short, slender fingers, while we stood aside. I went back very pleased that the girl was getting used to me.

Since it was quite cold at lunchtime, I lit a fire on the granary's earth floor, lay down beside it and slept for a little.

My brother came to wake me up. Prompted by his almost incoherent voice, I rushed out to the road, where the sun was still high.

'Li's calling,' he shouted, spittle spraying from the cor-ners of his mouth. 'He says he'll show everyone the soldier.'

'Soldier?' I shouted back, infected by his incoherence.

'The soldier; the runaway soldier.'

Pushing fiercely against his shoulder, I sped down the slope. Li was in the square in front of the school, his ruddy face, swollen like a ripe persimmon, growing redder and redder with excitement. Minami and the others were even more excited than Li.

'Really, a soldier?' I said to Li, my breath coming in gasps.

'Promise not to tell the villagers,' he said warily, filled with suspicion. 'You wouldn't break your word, you wouldn't betray me, would you?'

'Really, a soldier?' I repeated angrily.

'If you promise, don't anyone blab,' he said.

'I'm no squealer. We'd knock down any guy who did a thing like that,' I turned and roared to everyone.

'All right, everyone swear to keep their mouths shut.'

The group swore one and all to the binding strength of their oath. Minami, his voice shrill with exasperation and expectation, spoke as if almost threatening Li, who was still hesitating:

'You treat us like dogs: stop it, or we'll make you sorry.'

Making up his mind, Li nodded and, surrounding him, we ran down the road. He looked tense, as though he was already beginning to regret revealing his secret, hardly replying to our questions at all. But, persistently badgering him, we crossed the short bridge and went up the steep path to the Korean settlement. I remembered the army cadets standing ready by the truck and the murderous group of hunters from the village holding their bamboo spears, looking for the deserter. It must have been hard to evade their encirclement and escape across the valley.

'Where did you find the soldier?' I asked the group's incessant question once more in a strong voice, my arm round Li's shoulders. 'Go on, tell.'

'I don't really know,' he said, stammering. 'He's already been sheltering in our settlement for some time. During the day he sleeps in the abandoned mine, and at night he comes out to eat his meals.'

'So he's in the mine now?' inquired Minami.

'Now he's at my place, 'cos the villagers and the people from our settlement ran away.'

'What's he doing?' my brother said in an excited voice. 'Go on, what's he doing?'

'I'll show him to you now,' Li answered indignantly, then clamped his mouth shut.

The Korean settlement was made up of houses like sheds, even poorer and with even lower eaves than the village houses. Since there were no flagstones laid there, dust rose up from the parched earth. As the backs of the houses ran straight into the forest, the thick branches of the fir trees stretched out and overhung the road. Our throats dry with expectation, we marched obedient to Li, our steps rolling up the dust.

Li stopped at the end of the row of houses, in front of the warped, worm-eaten, double-boarded low door of the house where we had once seen the red flag, and we stopped too. Then he gave an inconspicuous little signal and went up the narrow path and round the back of the house. We waited. Suddenly the low door opened, and Li stuck his head out from the interior and summoned us in a sullen, grave voice.

'Come on in.'

We went in and saw, with eyes growing used to the darkness, a man who was lying on straw mats spread over the earth floor slowly lift his upper body. We all gazed at him, holding our breath, with some of us piled up on each other and peering in from outside as we couldn't all fit inside the house. The man looked back at Li, who was standing behind him. We stared blankly at his throat, sallow and covered with stubble, which was twitching in the darkness.

'Uh, it's all right' Li said, as if encouraging the man, 'They're friends. They said they won't squeal.'

The warm knot of expectation in my breast melted and bitter disappointment soaked through my body. The man had none of the sparkle, the lustre of an army cadet. He didn't have the small tight bum in uniform which excited desire, the brawny neck and bluish clean-shaven chin. Instead, he was glumly silent, showing a dark tired expression on a miserable shrivelled face of uncertain age. And instead of the sensual, totally obscene costume of war, he was wearing a work jacket.

'Everyone, have a quick look, then give the others a turn,' said Li, as though showing his friends a rabbit, and clearly wanting to put his 'rabbit' away quickly. 'He's tired. He doesn't want to be stared at for too long.'

The soldier silently lay back on the mat before our eyes. We went out, also in silence, changing places with our jostling comrades in the rear. Outside the air was fresh, unlike the atmosphere indoors, which was full of the odour of domestic animals. Sunk in disappointment, I breathed in the wind that smelled of tree bark.

But our younger comrades, their cheeks flushed, were excited and satisfied by seeing the deserter. They lined up to see the soldier again, behind those who were fretting and waiting their turn. I felt contempt for the boys who were discussing his escape admiringly together. I felt a dull unpleasant chill.

I signalled to my brother to come back to the village, but he was talking about the soldier with the others, his eyes shining. They were all bursting with excitement.

'The Koreans hid him,' one of them said, stammering with agitation. 'The police didn't understand them, because they talked together in Korean.'

'He got well away from the hunt,' another said. 'Those hunters can even catch wild boar.'

'He escaped,' my brother cried in a shrill voice. 'Escaped. . .'

Minami came out grumpily rubbing his fist on the seat of his pants. He and I went ahead back to the village. Minami spoke as he walked down the slope, pursing his lips in vexation.

'It's disgusting, he's really grubby; it's a real disappointment.'

'Even though he's an army cadet,' I said, 'he looks like a coward.'

'Yeah,' he said, 'I've never seen an army cadet like that.'

'Would you even sleep with him?'

'He'd be no use, just like a chicken.'

He scowled at me, showing his contempt and disgust, then laughed coldly. We waited on the bridge for my brother and the others to come down. But they were a long time coming.

'Anyway, I'll go and have a look,' Minami said suddenly, 'because it's bothering me.'

Even more angry, I saw him off as he ran up the slope, then squared my shoulders and went up the road to the square.

The girl was sitting in front of the warehouse hugging her knees. I went up to her to relieve my solitude. She looked at me in silence with her vague, grey-brown shadowed eyes. I leaned against the warehouse wall and we stared at each other for a while.

'Hey,' I said, swallowing saliva, 'you don't know about the deserter?'

The girl was silent and unresponsive.

'Well,' I said, shrugging my shoulders. 'Are you deaf and dumb?'

She lowered her eyes. The thick shadows of her lashes on her eyelids spread and turned blue like the shadows of leaves and grass.

'Come and have a meal at my place,' I said. 'Come on.

She raised her head vaguely. I bent over and grabbed her arm to try to make her stand up, then suddenly I was scratched with terrific force. Growing angry, I stood up and left straight away, leaving her there.

When I turned round in the square in front of the school, she was looking at me and following me like a cunning weasel. I was completely amazed, and disgusted. But it was good that she was coming. Pretending not to notice, I went back to the storehouse and waited for her.

When I was almost tired of waiting, the girl came quietly in behind my excited brother. He repeated enthusiastically that the deserter had at last come out of the house and had exchanged a few simple words with him and the others. The girl, sitting next to the fire on the earth floor with her head bowed, didn't even try to help cook the evening meal. I felt like bawling at her and my brother.

But once the meal began the three of us got on fine together. The girl chewed her food, gently moving the dirt-blackened scruff of her neck. Then she looked curiously at my brother, who was giving the dog food mouth-to-mouth.

'Hey, Brother,' he said suddenly, as an idea struck him, 'give my dog a name.'

'That's Bear,' said the girl.

I looked at the girl in surprise. She was flustered too. When my brother called out that name, the dog wagged his tail hard. My brother and I laughed happily, then the girl gave a bewildered little laugh. My good spirits restored, I went on laughing for a long time.

'Is this dog yours?' my brother asked, worried.

The girl shook her head.

'He's sweet, isn't he?' he said, relieved.

I wanted to say something to the girl as well, but I couldn't think of a good subject. What was more, my throat was itching and the words seemed to stick and wouldn't come out. So I gave up trying to speak and satisfied myself by putting fresh wood on the fire in front of her. As we were completely full, and the fire was hot and made our cheeks glow, the three of us and the dog were in a state of great contentment, apart from my brother talking about the deserter.

Next morning, we began our meal the same way by calling the girl from the warehouse. Afterwards, we went out into the square together. The girl sat silently on one side in the shadows of the trees, but she never tried to go back to the warehouse.

Chapter Six:
Love

In the afternoon the wind suddenly rose: the sky was clear, but the cold had deepened. The newly budding shrubs and the undergrowth of the leafless thickets on the mountainsides around the valley shook in the wind and sparkled brilliantly. We made a bonfire in the square in front of the school and gathered round it, sitting hugging our knees or walking round the square. The pale blue smoke of the bonfire, quickly dispersed by the wind, didn't reach the sky and as we had stared at the view of the village centred on the low bell-tower for so long that it was almost engraved on our memories, even gazing emptily at that scene was too boring. We had to spend the time not looking at anything, either just keeping still or walking around. Then we suddenly realized that we were worn out and edgy from living shut up in the village. The fatigue and indifference common to us all, the lack of endurance, were aspects of the mood that blanketed us.

However, when the soldier came into the square along with Li, the boys were roused and recovered their high spirits. The soldier also looked better than he had when we saw him yesterday in the dark house. But once he had slumped down in front of the bonfire he swept his weak eyes, bloodshot like a hare's, across our inquiring faces.

'We went to see the trolley track,' Li explained. 'As it is now, no one would come into the village from outside to catch him. We went to make sure.'

We realized that the soldier had benefited from the closure of the village. He lowered his eyes under our gaze.

'If you're caught. . .' my brother said to him timidly, but he kept silent.

'You'll be put on trial,' Li interceded.

'You'll be shot,' Minami said caustically. 'You'll be shot straight off.'

The soldier looked up at him with a tense expression. Minami was really angry. I expected the soldier to stir himself and knock him down, but he only stared at him like a child, clearly astonished.

'Huh,' Minami said, squaring his shoulders.

'This guy's good at escaping. He'll never be caught,' Li said.

'He won't get caught,' my brother said. 'You won't get caught, will you?'

The soldier looked at him. I felt that he had been comforted, but whenever I saw adults being consoled in that way it made me sick. So I sided with Minami's annoyance.

'When you were escaping, did you kill anyone?' another comrade asked.

'He didn't kill anyone; he didn't shoot either,' Li answered for him. 'Did you?'

'No,' the soldier spoke for the first time.

'He just didn't go back after going out,' Li said.

'You didn't want to go back, did you?' one of the comrades asked, blushing at the stupidity of his question.

The soldier was silent.

'I wanted to join the cadets,' the boy said, and there was a brief hush. A pensiveness charged with the desire for a cadet's uniform had seized us all.

'I didn't want to go to war,' the soldier suddenly said broodingly, 'I didn't want to kill people.'

This time a longer silence, a sense of intolerably uncomfortable discord, filled us. We had to hold back uncertain giggles that made our stomachs and backsides itch.

'I want to go to war and kill people,' said Minami.

'At your age you don't understand,' the soldier said, 'but then suddenly you do understand.'

We fell silent, half doubting him. It wasn't an interesting subject. The dog lying between my brother's legs abruptly got up and went over to sniff at the soldier's thin knees. He absent-mindedly stroked its head.

'Isn't he sweet?' my brother said, very happy. 'He's called Bear.'

'Leo is better,' said the soldier.

'Leo,' my brother said, after a brief pause. Then he avoided our reproachful gaze. 'I'll make it Leo, because it's my dog.'

I wanted to see if the girl, who was leaning against a mulberry tree at the corner of the square, had heard the dialogue about the dog's name, but I honestly couldn't tell. For me it was unpleasant that my brother should so readily give up the dog's name that she had taught him.

'Leo,' my brother repeated dreamily.

'You were a student, weren't you?' said Minami.

'Yeah,' said the soldier. 'A student of the humanities.'

'I thought so,' Minami said scornfully. 'A student who lived near my house gave a cat that kind of name.'

The soldier, clearly nonplussed, looked as though he was trying to ignore Minami's persistent baiting. I left them and went to the girl, who was sitting at the base of the mulberry tree.

'He was scared of the war and ran away,' I said to her. She stayed silent. 'I hate cowards. When I'm near him, there's a stink. You hate him too, don't you?'

The girl looked up at me, bewildered, then gave a weak smile. Disgruntled, I went back to the granary, whistling.

That night the moon shone brightly. Since my brother had gone with Li to the Korean settlement to have dinner with the soldier, taking the dog along, the girl and I had to eat porridge by ourselves. Then we spent a long time in silence warming our hands by the fire on the earth floor, letting our stomachs work in peace. From time to time birds cried shrilly in the forest. I was a little annoyed that my brother was so obsessed with the deserter. I yawned and shed little tears, and that spread to the girl. She gave a small yawn, pushing out her tightly clenched fists in front of her. She looked so very tired.

'Are you sleepy?' I asked.

'Yeah,' she said weakly.

'I'm not sleepy,' I said.

The girl's grape-coloured hair twined around her thin neck. Her whole body gave off a smell like musty straw. I thought calmly that her skin was no cleaner than mine. We were silent again for a long time. I began to worry that my brother hadn't come home.

'Hey,' the girl said, turning her small dark face towards me.

'Yeah?' I said, surprised.

'I'm scared.'

'Of course you're scared; it's not surprising.'

'I'm scared,' she said, twisting her lips as if about to cry.

'Are you scared of staying in the village, of children staying alone in the village.'

'I'm scared.'

'Everyone's scared,' I said in a huff. 'We're scared, but there's nothing we can do, is there? Because we're cut off.'

'Bring back the villagers,' she said imploringly.

Perplexed, I was silent.

'Please, call them back,' she repeated.

'I can't do that,' I said harshly. 'We got cut off.'

'I'm scared,' she said and started to sob, burying her face between her knees. I stubbornly ignored her and kept quiet, but the girl, continually crying in a soft voice, made me more and more uncomfortable and irritated me.

'If I go and call the villagers, they won't come back,' I said. 'And if they do come back, they'll catch the soldier and kill him.'

She went on sobbing inconsolably. An insane feeling grew inside me. Biting my lip, I stood up and took the map which the doctor had given me out of my kit-bag. The trolley track crossing the valley and the route to the doctor's house were roughly sketched in it.

'I'll tell them to come and just fetch you,' I said brusquely to the girl, who was looking up, her face blotched with tears. 'I'll go and tell that to the guys on the other side of the valley. Stop blubbering.'

I went out on the road, which was bright under the moon. The fog was drifting, harsh and chill. The girl followed me outside, but I didn't look back. I didn't even know whether I could reach the other side of the valley or not. But in any case, I wanted to hand over the girl, whose little face was wet with tears and whose whole body stank, to the bunch on the other side. I couldn't bear it.

As I came out of the forest, the trolley track, dripping from the fog, shone in the moonlight. Then the black looming mass of the barricade. The light in the hut on the far side where the guard should be keeping watch had been put out. I turned back and spoke to the girl, who was biting her lips that were blue with cold.

'Wait here; I'll talk to them about you.'

When I stepped onto the track's sleepers, taking care not to slip, the fog and a sharp chill came blowing up from beneath them, striking my cheeks and stinging my nostrils. Far below, the water current shining in the moonlight and the sound of it gnawing the rocks made a swirling motion. Slowly, hunched over like a beast, I went on walking over the sleepers. My excitement soon subsided. I thought what I was doing was nothing special. But I had no intention of going back. So I half-closed my eyes to keep them from being hurt by the hard bitter wind and focused all my attention on stepping on the dead centre of each sleeper.

The track was very long and the wind was fierce. By the time I reached the barricade, piled with treestumps, bundles of sticks, boards and chunks of rock, I was so tired that

I wanted to lay down and sleep, and my throat was dry. I verified that the barricade was too heavy and complicated for me to remove, but that if I climbed over it, it would collapse immediately. I peered at the underside of the sleepers. There was no other way. First I straightened up and put my frozen hands inside my trousers and in my groin to warm them. As my fingers gradually recovered their senses, they felt the presence of my penis, shrunken and wrinkled with cold and fear.

Placing my elbows on the sleepers, I curled up and slid my legs through the narrow gap. The next moment, I was hanging from the sleepers by both hands, exposing my whole body to the valley's icy void. The harsh wind and cold, and a terrible loneliness, assailed me. I had to fight them. Twisting my body haphazardly like a shrimp simmering in tepid water, I swung from one sleeper to the next.

My strength almost exhausted, I put my hands on the last sleeper and, with a gasp that was almost a scream, chinned up, put my elbows on its upper surface which was covered with crystalline frost, and lifted my body. I stretched out on top of the sleepers and panted for breath. But I couldn't lay there in full view in the moonlight. If I was shot at from the guard hut, my head would be smashed by the first bullet. Exhaling harsh gasps, I walked over the sleepers for the last short distance and when I reached firm ground I ran up the slope beside the dark bushes, staying out of the moonlight. Then, without even having to take the map from my breast pocket and look at it, I went through a sparse woodland of oaks and chestnuts planted together in a jumble, and there in front of me was a smallish village, peaceful in the moonlight. It appeared suddenly, in the same way that every other farming community had appeared so far.

I went down the sloping road spotted with rounded stones and into the village. It was made up of houses, trees along the roadside and winding alleys that were almost the same as those in the village where we were imprisoned. But there was a subtle difference in the air in this village, and that scared me. People were living there. Strangers were living there. The village was quiet and I felt the stirring of domestic animals from the interiors, the dark cold interiors, of the houses. I went on walking between the low-eaved houses, casting a small shadow in the moonlight. The strangers who had cut us off and stood guard over us were sleeping in those houses. Fear and a violent surge of excitement made waves of shivering race over my frost-nipped skin. To suppress the urge to run away as fast as I could, I concentrated on searching for the doctor's house.

I knocked on the Western-style door of the doctor's house, which was fitted with pocked and bubbled panes of glass. Then, stepping back a pace, right into the moonlight, I watched the door with its glass panes, so rare in the village. A light went on behind it, a figure came up to the entrance, mumbling in its throat, and the small animal-like head of the doctor I had seen at the warehouse poked out from the slightly opened door. We eyed each other very warily. I thought in consternation that I must say something, but I was choked up and almost crying.

'Well,' said the doctor in a voice that made my softened feelings suddenly harden. 'What have you come here for?'

I was silent, staring at him wide-eyed. His plump cheeks and small nose were filled with something like fear, and that hardened my heart still further.

'You, what have you come here for? If you get violent, I'll call someone.'

'I won't get violent,' I said in an excited, thickened voice, curbing my anger. 'I didn't come here for that.'

'What did you come for?' he repeated.

'The village girl was left behind in the warehouse. She wants to get out of the village. You, take her out, please.'

The doctor looked me over searchingly. I saw his bared gums soaked and glistening with saliva, and cunning spread quickly from there all over his face. I repeated hastily:

'Please, come and do it.'

'How many of you have contracted the disease? How many of you are left alive?' he asked.

'What?' I said in surprise. 'We're not ill; the girl's fine too. There's no plague.'

He looked at me more carefully.

'If you think I'm lying, take a look at me. I'll undress so you can examine me.'

'Don't speak so loud,' said the doctor. 'Who said I'd take a look at you.'

I lowered my hand from my coat buttons, which I had almost undone to bare my upper body in the moonlight. He wouldn't listen to me at all.

'You're a doctor, aren't you? It's your job to see if someone's ill or not, isn't it?'

'Don't be impudent,' he said, suddenly showing anger. 'Go back; don't come over to this side again.'

'I thought you'd tell everyone that there's no plague

going round. You're a doctor,' I said, flushed all over with indignation. 'But you're sending me back?'

'Go back!' he said. 'If the villagers find out, you'll pay for it. You'll get me into trouble. Go back!'

I squared my shoulders defiantly. The doctor came out in front of me from behind the door, wearing a stiff gown like an animal skin.

'Go back, don't come here again,' he said, quickly twisting my arm and speaking in a voice filled with anger. Letting out a little groan from the pain, I struggled to break free from his strong grip, but he stood there firmly, solid as a rock.

'If the villagers find you wandering around here, you won't survive,' he said. 'I'll make you go back.'

His hand grabbed the scruff of my neck. I had to start walking, dragged along by him, not even able to squirm. I was burning with anger. But it was hard to release myself from that humiliating position. The doctor hurried me along, almost shaking me.

'You're disgusting; you're supposed to be a doctor and you won't try to help us,' I said, my voice thin and high-pitched, squeezed out from my throat.

The doctor's hand squeezed harder, and I groaned with pain. I was dragged along like that. Finally I was thrown down in front of the trolley track. Fallen on the cold ground, I looked up at the doctor's stocky body, looming black against the background of the dark forest. It was filled with overbearing strength and authority.

'You're just going to watch us die,' I said. I felt ashamed that my voice was so weak and fearful, but to lie there in silence would have been more shameful. 'You're vile.'

The doctor bent down, and a terrific impact struck my

back as though I had been hit by a heavy stone. I cried out and writhed away, rolling over to avoid his foot, drawn back for the next kick. Vindictively, he tried to pursue me. Screaming with fear, I crawled down to the trolley track and started moving along it.

I was completely exhausted. But when I saw the doctor bend down to pick up a stone to throw at me, I knew I couldn't stay there. I crawled along the track, clawing at the sleepers with panicky fingers, then when I reached the barricade I slid my legs, trembling with rage in that shameful posture, under the track.

When I lifted my body up onto the trolley track again after the arduous struggle, using almost all the strength that I had left to do a last chin-up, I could only pant violently, my chest rising and falling like a tormented beast. Then I was mad with a desperate fury. My fingertips were lacerated and bleeding. I thought I heard someone's footsteps receding behind me, but instead of turning round, I gazed at the end of the long track illuminated by the moon. The girl was looking at me, her small head peeping out from behind the winch apparatus.

I stood up and walked across on the sleepers, forcing my wobbly knees into action. When my feet touched the other side, the earth on that side where we were definitely shut in, the girl jumped out, staring at me with wide eyes that shone like those of a feverish child. We stared at each other like that for a long time. Anger raged over my body. Breathing hard, I tore myself free from her pressing, entangling gaze and started to walk. She followed me hastily, but I went on walking briskly without slackening my pace.

Those pigs, those bloody pigs, I shouted to myself as I

walked. The back of my neck tingled with pain where I had been grabbed. The doctor's baseness, his bestial strength and my weakness. I couldn't do anything about those pigs. I quickened my pace to stop my helpless indignation and my sorrow mingling with my rage. Now the girl was trotting and panting. As she panted, she went on mumbling something over and over again, but I didn't even try to catch it.

We passed through the forest, went down the paved road that was bright in the moonlight, passed between the houses where our sleeping comrades lay and came out in front of the girl's warehouse. She stopped and I stopped. Then we stared at each other again. Tears had gathered in her swollen, bloodshot eyes and they reflected the moonlight, sparkling. Now her thin lips were moving without emitting a sound. Suddenly the meaning of the words they had been repeating became clear to me.

I thought you wouldn't come back, they said over and over again. I thought you wouldn't come back; they cried out the words, interspersed with senseless convulsive spasms. I turned my eyes away from her lips and looked down at my sore fingers. The blood was dripping onto the paving stones. Suddenly the girl's hand reached out, then she bent down and took my fingers between her lips, and her hard tongue, moving in little darts, probed my wounds repeatedly and moistened them with sticky saliva. The nape of her neck, rounded and pliant as a pigeon's back, was moving slightly under my bowed head.

A feeling swelled up inside me, then suddenly ballooned and went right to my head. I grabbed the girl's shoulders roughly and pulled her up. I no longer saw the expression on her small upturned face. I hugged her like a cornered, panicky chicken and ran with her into the darkened warehouse.

We went straight into the completely dark interior, and I silently dropped my trousers and lifted her skirt: I threw myself down on the girl's body. I groaned as my erect penis, like an asparagus stalk, caught in my underpants and was almost bent double. Then contact with the cold, dry, papery surface of her sex, and withdrawal with little shivers. I sighed deeply.

That was all. I stood up and put on my trousers, fumbling, then went outside, leaving the girl lying there breathing unsteadily. Outside, the cold was rapidly intensifying and the moonlight poured its mineral hardness down on the trees and paving stones. I was still insanely angry and frenzied mumbling filled my mouth, but a rich sensation filled with sweetness slowly raised its head from beneath all that. As I ran up the slope my eyes filled with tears and I tensed the muscles of my face to stop them flowing down my cheeks.

Chapter Seven:

The Hunt and the Festival in the Snow

At daybreak I was wakened by the bitter cold, but I kept my eyes tight shut. The elation stirring in my breast, my heated passion filled me from within and closed me up tight from outside. Why is it, what's the cause of this strange tension, I wondered. But the drowsiness that lingered, buoyant and restless, deep inside my head and throughout my body, hampered my thoughts. I opened my eyes a little and stared at my fingers in the cold air that was filled with a stronger, sharper radiance than the usual dawn. The wounds opened, soft and rosy. The darting, sensitive tip of the pigeon-like girl's tongue had touched them again and again, moistening them with sticky saliva. Like boiling water, love suddenly soaked every inch of my body right down to my fingertips. After a shiver of satisfaction I curled up again and tried to immerse myself in the dregs of sleep. But the exaltation that had caught hold of me wouldn't go away. The twittering of innumerable birds that I had hardly ever heard before blew in from outside like a tempest. And it seemed as if an enormous heavy silence was lying underneath it all. I got up, moved the draught-excluding mat and peeped out through the narrow chink.

Outside there was an entirely new, pure dawn. Snow had piled up and covered the earth, giving the trees the rounded profile of beasts' shoulders, and it was shining in a vast brightness. Snow, I thought, letting out a deep sigh. I've never seen such abundance, such lavish snow, in my life. The birds were chirping furiously. But the thick layers of snow absorbed every other sound. The birdsong and the immense silence. I was all alone in a wide world and love had just been born. I groaned with pleasure and rocked back and forth. Then, like a joyful giant, I went down on one knee, biting my lip and with tears in my eyes, I gazed at the snow outside. I couldn't stay silent.

I turned and called excitedly to my brother, who was sleeping deeply.

'Hey, wake up, wake up.'

He twisted his shoulders, groaning deep in his throat, then slowly opened his eyes. They were chestnut brown and shining brightly, then they quietly and softly melted. He was having a nightmare, I thought. And he must have been comforted straight away when he saw me looking at him as he awoke.

'Get up,' I said.

'Yeah,' he said, sitting up, the dirty skin of his knees showing through the rips in his trousers.

'Look,' I shouted, smartly pulling away the mat. 'Look at this snow.'

The outdoors, with its tremendous breadth and space, came rushing in. Hearing my brother's cheers, I slid open the glass door and thrust my head out. Thick chunks of snow blew over me, warm on my skin. I twisted my shoulders and looked up at the sky, and the ashen brownish snow was falling softly and incessantly, faster and faster.

'Ah,' my brother said in a shrill voice, trembling with his shoulder pushed against my hip. 'It really came down while I was asleep.'

'Just like this, while you were asleep,' I said, patting his shoulder. 'I slept for a long time too.'

'A hundred years?' he said, laughing breathlessly. 'I've a hundred years' worth of pissing to do.'

'Me too,' I shouted, swiftly moving my fingers.

The snow had made a high drift just outside the glass door. We urinated on its purity, our penises side by side, shrivelled in the cold, and the honey-coloured stains on the snow melted slowly and sank in. I looked down at my cock, and recalled the feel of the cold, dry, papery surface of the girl's sex. A sensation of healthy delight ran tingling beneath my skin. Me and my small erect penis were both filled with youthful vitality.

An agile shape sprang up in the snowfield, scattering the fine snowflakes, and came closer and closer. 'Leo,' my brother shouted in a sharp voice and at almost the same moment the dog jumped up at him and pushed him back on the ground.

Leo rolled around, shaking his body over and over again and plastering his fur with snow, licked my brother's neck and cheeks and nipped his shoulders and arms.

My brother shrieked excitedly with laughter and grappled with his dog as he yapped, finally pinning him down.
The dog whined feebly in a wheedling voice and my
brother looked up at me with moist, smiling eyes. I and
my brother, who was breathing deeply with his chest rising and falling, stared smiling at each other's eyes for a
really long time.

I wound cloth rags round my brother's short neck,
then while he went back into the straw and blankets
again, cuddling the dog, I lit a fire with the piled-up
wood on the earth floor and grilled some dried fish.
There was plenty of food left for us, and if we dug away
the snow we could find plenty of fat stems of watery
Chinese cabbage quietly hidden away. I put the pot of
cold hard porridge on the piled-up firewood and dropped
in a handful of snow that I grabbed from outside. After a
while the lump of snow, which had retained the imprint
of my fingers, crumbled and sank in the lively rising
steam. When I turned round to get some more wood to
add to the fire, my brother, who I thought had fallen
asleep, was staring at my back in silence.

'What?' I asked, slightly bewildered. 'Are you and the
dog awake?'

'The dog sneaked out,' he said, smiling. 'You didn't
notice, did you?'

'No,' I said.

'I trained him,' he said.

'Get up and eat.'

'I'll wash my face in the snow,' he said, tying the string of
his trousers.

'You can do it later.'

Taking his mess tin out of his kit-bag, he spoke in a low

childish voice. 'Let's stay here always, for a long time, like this.'

'You and I'll turn into ignorant stupid grown-ups,' I said. But like my brother, I too had begun to wish to live a long life in this house surrounded by snow. And every last exit was closed to us. What more could we want than this? I absolutely refused to relive last night's humiliation.

After breakfast, when my brother and I went outside with the smell of grilled dried fish hanging around our faces, the snow and wind had already ceased, and the sky had cleared to a dazzling blue. The snow covering the ground, the trees and the houses was shining brilliantly. Birdsong swept over us like fresh wind, like fresh snow. We walked over the snow which covered our heels, with our shoulders pressed together.

Our comrades were gathered in the square in front of the school. Then I saw the girl a little further away, almost leaning against the wet black trunk of an old chestnut tree that wore the snow like a hat. My brother and I ran down the slope, shouting and kicking the snow about. The boys greeted us, calling in reply. Once I had run up to them, it was hard for me to turn my face towards the chestnut tree, as I was stopped by a hot feeling which suddenly welled up inside.

'You and the soldier are the only ones who slept this late,' Minami said, his eyes sparkling. 'We've been working here since before dawn.'

'Working?' I shouted back to shake off my physical discomfort towards the chestnut tree.

'We thought about skating, and we're making a skating rink.'

Prompted by the words 'skating rink', heavy with nostalgia gnawing at our hearts like fire, we all laughed madly. The snow on the slope had hardened and the middle was frozen over with a colour like hard celluloid. Some slid on it unsteadily, and others pounded the snow with boards wrapped in cloth to widen and lengthen the narrow track. Everyone had bright red cheeks and strong white breath. After a short run-up I launched myself on the frozen snow-covered slope that was shining in the sun and straightaway tumbled over hard. My brother was floundering beside me like a clumsy bear cub. I got up, wiping the snow from my back and bum, before my jeering comrades' smiling faces, then, biting my lip, I walked straight over to the chestnut tree.

The girl smiled as she watched me approach, her face flushed. Beneath her thin skin, with its pale egg-coloured gloss, fine blotches of blood floated up then sank back again, following the rhythm of the struggle between her smile and the cold.

'Were you surprised it snowed like this?' I said after quickly moistening my lips with my tongue.

'I'm used to this much snow,' she said earnestly, squaring her shoulders.

'Ah?' I said uncertainly, then we laughed in unison.

I recovered my composure, and was now convinced and satisfied that I was once again immersed in this, my first love. When I turned round with the girl by my side, pushing my back against the trunk, my comrades were staring at us in amazement. I smiled at them indulgently. I burned with joy as I felt the girl's right wrist rub hesitantly against my left hand.

Minami whistled to taunt us. I answered him with a very

friendly smile, which spread to all my comrades, Minami included. Once they understood fully that there had been physical relations between me and the girl, they no longer showed any interest in us and concentrated instead on their own activities. They tumbled over, laughing and yelling. My brother was excluded from the games because Leo, who was hanging around him, would scratch the hardened snow with his claws, so he sat down next to us embracing the dog's back, and gazed happily at the sliding on the snow.

'Do your fingers hurt?' asked the girl, quickly craning up to my ear.

'They don't hurt at all,' I said with dignity.

'You're brave,' she said. 'You're pretty brave for your age.'

'For my age?' I said, unable to suppress my laughter and worrying in case that laugh had offended her. 'Who told you my age?'

'Well, if you look at really broad age groups,' said the girl simply. 'There are children and adults, and babies as well, aren't there? Those kinds of age groups.'

I felt a little contemptuous towards the girl and deliberately laughed out loud, then bent over and stroked the dog's neck. My brother held onto its hindquarters, but he was completely fascinated by our comrades' sliding.

'You understand?' my lover said, a little bashfully. Then she took a paper parcel from her jacket and halved the food tightly wrapped inside it: pastry baked hard as stone. She silently gave me the slightly larger half and pressed with her thumbs hard to break the remainder in two. I was about to move my right hand, which was resting on the dog, back to my knee to halve my share for my brother.

At that moment the dog jumped up and bit the girl's wrist, which was stretched out just above his head. She screamed, and Leo ran off up the slope, taking his booty, which had dropped onto the snow, in his mouth. The girl pressed her injured right hand against her lips. I thought of her nimble tongue wetting her tender wound, then recalled the sensation of that tongue on my injured fingers and the burning passion of my love. Inside my head there was the sound of boiling blood.

'Does it hurt?' I said, putting my hand on her shoulder. 'Show me.'

But the girl, holding her wound to her mouth, didn't answer. Then her cheeks suddenly lost colour, closed up in fear, and with the reddish-black stains that rose to the surface she looked rather ugly. My comrades came running up and surrounded us. A furious rage seized me. My brother turned pale and, after hesitating, ran up the slope after Leo.

'Hey, it hurts, doesn't it?' I said. 'Well? How is it?'

Leaving my comrades behind, I took the girl back in silence with my arm around her shoulders. In front of the warehouse she suddenly shook off my arm and ran into the dark entrance. So I just went back. I was angry and despairing. I didn't want to do anything. But I joined in the sliding on the snow, yelling.

In fact, the sliding was really enjoyable. It was enjoyable enough to make the girl and my anger and despair vanish from my mind by around noon, when my skin had become sweaty under my shirt.

When I grew really hungry I went back up the slope for a meal. My brother was sitting disconsolately inside the dark entrance that blocked out the sun, holding the dog against his knees. That shook me.

'I scolded the dog,' he said, hanging his head. 'I really scolded him.'

He's upset, I thought, and said generously, 'It doesn't matter. That girl's exaggerating.'

And once I'd said that, it seemed it really didn't matter. Who would lay the blame on a dog and his young keeper, a guilt so heavy that they must sit in the dark indoors with bowed heads on a snowy afternoon?

We ate the leftovers from breakfast standing on the earth floor and gave some to Leo. While we were eating we couldn't wait to get back outside again for the sliding.

But no one spent that afternoon sliding on the snow. Li had come down from the forest cradling in his brawny well-muscled arms two pigeons, a shrike and two small birds whose beautiful backs had chestnut ripples against dark-brown plumage, along with a small trap. The birds in Li's arms were splendidly elegant with their tight-shut eyes.

We were thrilled almost to distraction as we made traps following Li's example and, assembling late that afternoon like an invading army, we went into the forest. Inside the coppiced woodland Li gave loud instructions and then we scattered, each going his own way, carried away by the birdsong.

My brother and I were holding small traps patiently knotted together from hemp fibres to lay on the snow-dusted grass before scattering grain and waiting for the birds to entangle their thin hard legs — a bunch of smallish cunning traps — and a woven bamboo basket. We first set a hempen trap in a little hollow where frozen grass blades peeped out from the snow, then withdrew, erasing our footprints. The trap spread its mesh over the coarse-grained, already freezing snow, and when I looked at it I could feel with my own body the birds entangling their sharp-clawed legs in the mesh, crying piercingly and struggling, scattering feathers and a smell tinged with blood. My throat flushed. I thumped my brother's shoulder enthusiastically and he laughed, showing his pink gums between dry lips.

We had to choose a place to set up the bamboo basket. And in addition, we had to stay where we could hear the flapping of struggling birds caught in the trap. According to Li, if we left them even for only a short time, the other birds would be alerted and hungry animals would snatch our prey. He stressed that if this happened it would endanger hunts in the future.

Ah, future hunts. Labouring heroically, my brother and I set the basket among some oak trees, where a thick layer of dead leaves beneath the snow felt soft underfoot, and propped it up with a dead twig. We then tied a long string to the prop and ran it out to a hawthorn bush. We would watch a pigeon as it ate the grains beneath the bamboo basket and as soon as its blue-grey head had gone inside the basket we would pull the string with all our might. The pigeon would struggle in our arms — thrust into the basket by digging through the snow — and would bring up a little blood as its neck was wrung.

My brother and I crouched in a thicket of chest-high deciduous shrubs that were armed with short hairs and thorns, and watched our trap. The birds were singing high in the treetops and when I looked up, I saw a pale blue winter sky, incredibly high above the entangled tree branches. I pricked up my ears, but apart from my brother's breathing and the birdsong, and the occasional heavy sound of snow falling, there was a terrifyingly massive silence, and I couldn't hear my comrades' voices. Whenever I noticed that I was becoming absorbed in dark sombre thoughts, I shook myself to dispel them. I had no intention of disclosing last night's humiliation to anyone, including my brother. The birds didn't come for ages.

'My bum's getting wet,' my brother said. 'The snow's soaking in.'

We had sat down on dry fallen leaves which we had spread over the snow, to await the arrival of the birds. I stood up and went to collect dry dead leaves under the trees. When I dug down there was deep, clear water flowing through the dead leaves and fresh whitish-blue buds swelling, which astonished me. And insect pupae wrapped in their shells.

Sitting on the newly spread fallen leaves, my brother watched the trap eagerly. I and Leo, who was pressing his shoulder against my brother's knee, stared at his swollen red chilblained hands which clutched the string like a deadly weapon.

The birds didn't come for a really long time. Leo, my brother and I were drawn into the gentle, deep-seated gyrations of time which revolved around the trap; my brother and I yawned, our eyes filled with tears, and the dog moved his ears nervously. The unease and drowsiness which by now had become normal began gradually soaking into me.

My brother sighed.

'What's the matter?' I asked, making a fist.

'I thought a big bird flew down from the branches,' he said with a gentle smile on his sleepy childish face, 'because a little wedge-shaped leaf dropped right in front of my eyes.'

I stood up and spoke quickly to him. 'I'll go back down for a bit.'

'Are you going to that girl who looks like a pigeon?' he said, little wrinkles gathering round his eyes.

'Yeah. I'll go and apologize about Leo.'

I ran down the slope, scattering snow. The dead branches of the shrubs — a kind of rose — snapped off as my hips brushed them, and Leo, who followed me for a short time, picked one up in his mouth and went back to my brother.

It was cold inside the warehouse, and stuffy with the smell of bare earth, moss and tree bark. I opened the wooden door and stayed where I was for a while to let my eyes grow used to the darkness. It seemed like I needed rather a long time, because outside it had been very bright with the sun reflecting on the snow everywhere. Then the girl's small face appeared — red with fever and with the down from her cheeks to her ears shining golden. She sat in the middle of the earth floor with a thin quilt wrapped round her neck. Gazing at her eyes, which were like those of a baby animal, I slowly closed the door.

'You're cold, aren't you?' I said in a hoarse voice.

'Yeah,' she said, knitting her brows.

As for me, I was sweaty under my shirt from running. Now I couldn't remember what I had wanted to happen in the warehouse while I was running, and I was irritated.

'Are you ill?' I asked, flummoxed by my own question. I wondered if the girl thought I was stupid.

'I don't know,' she answered coolly, making me more ashamed.

'Is there anything I can do?'

'Light the fire.'

I recovered my courage and, bustling about smartly, I threw firewood into the hearth cut into the earth floor and made a fire, choking in the smoke. The girl's face looked drained and lifeless in the orange light, like a rather stupid child. And the skin round her mouth was dry and etched with many whitish lines.

I sat down on the wooden floor and watched her from across the fire. The fact that I had made the fire put me more at ease, but I also felt that if someone had opened the door and come in I would have dashed out in great confusion. And I thought that I needed to say something important to her, but my throat was dry and the words wouldn't come.

'I want to have a pee,' she said, suddenly filled with authority, 'but I can't get up properly.'

'I'll lift you,' I said, my face flooding with blood, 'I'll hold your shoulders.'

She peeled the quilt off her torso by herself and revealed her body, clad in a neat red flannel nightie that I hadn't seen before. I looked down at her small trembling chest then helped her up, holding her surprisingly hot shoulders. We marched round to the other side of the wooden partition in silence, then I turned round and waited for her, holding my breath.

'I've finished,' she said with greater authority, and I carried her back.

After lying down and pulling the quilt up to her chest she screwed up her face as though annoyed and closed her eyes. That worried me. But I thought I'd better not speak to her.

'My feet are cold and sore,' she said with her eyes still closed. 'They really hurt.'

I hesitantly slipped my hands under the end of the quilt and rubbed her calves and ankle joints, which were as hard as the nodes of a young tree.

'You can take the quilt off. Warm your hands at the fire and rub me,' she ordered.

The red nightie was short and a little dirty, but it exposed her lithe well-shaped knees without even the tiniest scar. I rubbed zealously and vigorously. The blood slowly came back into her calves and started flowing, perhaps even with a faint noise. I thought about my knees, covered by thick coarse-grained skin with many scars, and sighed over hers, which were like smooth flesh stretching down from her inner thighs. The girl, silent and motionless, gave her legs up to me and didn't tell me to stop for a long time. Her calves grew warm in my hands and reminded me of the birds' bodies still warm in Li's arms. Then, baffled by anguish which burned my chest like fire, I felt my penis quietly harden.

'If you want to,' the girl said in a shrill childish voice that caught in her throat, 'you can see my tummy.'

I wrapped her feet in the quilt roughly and stood up. I was really confused.

'I'm going home,' I shouted angrily at her and myself, and ran out of the warehouse.

But as I ran into the forest, where my brother was watching from amongst the hardy rose shrubs, I was almost mad with the pride and joy that welled up inside me. Unknown to anyone, I had a sweet and marvellous lover.

Breathless, I ran through the snow-crowned trees to my own virile hunt, often slipping as I climbed the slope, hearing the snow fall right behind me.

Emitting white panting breath, I stuck my head through the wet branches and looked at the trap on the snow. But there were not even any feathers tangled in the hempen mesh, and the grain was still where we had scattered it. I tut-tutted and tried to get to where my brother's trap was, crossing through the thicket. Then I heard flurried, powerful wingbeats and a dog's barking in the cedar wood far up on the right-hand side. I ran up hastily.

The cedar wood was dark and damp, and its thick air resisted my passage. The dog's barking and the wingbeats arose from the faint brightness on the other side of the wood. I advanced towards it, chafing my legs on the ferns. One corner where the cedars had been felled was bright with snow mounds, and there I saw my brother and the dog struggling on the ground. Then louder wingbeats and my brother rolling about.

I ran up and saw that he was holding on to a magnificent pheasant.

'Hey, kill it,' I shouted.

The dog barked and the sound of the bird's neckbone breaking rang out softly, then it collapsed limply on my brother's chest.

'Hey,' I cried, my voice warm with surprise. 'Hey, you. . .'

He jumped up, peeling back his pale trembling lips, holding the pheasant firmly against his chest and, gazing at me hard as if his eyes were shaken by fits, he thrust his body against mine. I hugged his shoulders and patted him on the back. He growled wordlessly, his whole body trembling.

'Hey, you did it,' I shouted with joy, almost overwhelmed by the urge to sob.

'Yeah,' my brother said in a low hoarse voice, pressing his face against my chest.

We hugged each other like that for a little while. Leo ran round us barking, then suddenly jumped up. My brother let go of me, threw the pheasant down and grappled with Leo. They rolled around on the snow. Then I joined in the scuffle. We were poisoned with madness in every vein.

Suddenly my brother slumped down exhausted and, with my arm entangled with his, I also sat down on the snow. Leo jumped on the pheasant and carried it to his master's knees. We gazed at it silently for a long time. My brother's finger stroked the hard green feathers with a reddish gloss on the crown of its head, then its dark violet neck wet with the dog's saliva and its back, overflowing with rich colours. It was beautiful, tightly packed and filled with life.

I saw that there were tears running down my brother's cheeks, and that his neck was covered with scratches.

'You got done in, really done in,' I said, dusting snow off his body.

My brother looked up at me, eyes shining with tears, and laughed shriekingly in short bursts. Then we stood up and staggered back through the cedars to the coppiced woodland. All the while, my brother talked about his brave hunt, rambling on, occasionally possessed by laughter as if swollen to bursting point with emotion or shaken by fits. He hugged the pheasant, digging his nails into its flesh.

While he was watching the trap from the thicket, Leo had chased a pheasant out of the snow-ringed grass and had bitten its wing. My brother had chased the pheasant, to help Leo, but had lost it in front of the cedar wood. I was so ashamed that I almost cried, he said. When he had tried to go back to his trap, Leo had jumped up vigorously and chased out the pheasant, which had lost its powers of flight and was hiding in the ferns. My brother had grappled with it and, despite being beaten by its gigantic strong wings, had at last triumphed.

'Look,' he said, tossing his head. 'My right eye got hurt really badly; I still can't see properly.'

It was really bloodshot and looked like an over-ripe apricot. I grabbed my brother's head and shook it, mimicking his laughter.

Yelling, we ran to the square in front of the school where the others were standing round Li displaying their catch. My brother's prey immediately became the focus of every young hunter's admiration and envy. The pheasant, expanding and shining golden in my comrades' unanimous adulation, completely filled the village in the valley. My brother ecstatically repeated the story of his adventure, wriggling with short excited laughter that from time to time became just a scarcely comprehensible growling noise.

'You're terrific,' said Li, looking at him with eyes filled with friendship.

My brother threw the pheasant down on the snow in his great joy at Li's tribute. And when Minami came back, having caught one small white-eye, we jeered at him. Minami was really mortified, but in front of the pheasant, with its gentle gloss in the burning gold and orange evening light, his tiny green bird looked like a handful of dirt about to crumble, which even he had to admit.

Clicking his tongue, Minami threw his white-eye down on the snow and the other comrades followed suit. A surge of excitement arose, charged with the spirit of the pile on the snow that was decked in soft grey-blue, black and yellow, green and whitish-brown feathers, centring on the superb pheasant.

'We're going to have a festival in our village on this day we caught our first pheasant,' Li said. 'That'll ensure the success of our future hunts. The thing is, there aren't any villagers here right now, so they won't have a festival. If we don't do it, the hunts'll all go wrong and the village will decline.'

'Let's do it,' I said. 'We'll ensure the success of our hunts for the village.'

'Our village?' Minami said, twisting his lips. 'Is it? We were abandoned.'

'It's our village,' I said, glaring at him. 'I've never been abandoned by anyone.'

'All right then,' he said, with a crafty grin. 'I like festivals.'

'Do you know how to do it?' I asked Li. 'How to do the festival?'

'We'll cook the birds here and eat them,' he said. 'We'll sing and dance, and the festival'll go fine like that. It's always been that way.'

'Let's do it,' I said, and the comrades cheered. 'Let's have our festival.'

'Everyone, go and get firewood and food,' said Li. 'I'll get a big cooking pot.'

The comrades ran yelling back to their houses, and I grabbed my brother by the shoulder and ran up the slope to fetch the firewood.

'I'll teach you the festival song,' Li was shouting, swinging his arms. 'We'll sing until morning.'

Chapter Eight:
Sudden Outbreak of Disease and Panic

Once we had gathered green wood, which gave off a smell impregnated with carnal sweetness from sharp axe cuts, carried it to the school's broad earth floor, hung up a pot-hook and fixed a big cooking pot to it, the axis of the festival was established. We threw the firewood down, stuck dry twigs into it and lit a fire. The oily water in the pot, with coarsely chopped dried fish floating in it, soon began to bubble. The soldier, who had come as a result of Li's persistent entreaties, rolled his sleeves up his thin arms and stirred the pot.

We plucked the birds and laid their obscene naked swollen-bellied bodies on the snow. Li singed them over the fire one at a time to burn off their soft down, and a slight odour of meat wafted to our nostrils. Some of the birds revived unexpectedly as they were having their necks wrung and squirmed violently, and that stirred us into laughter. We wrenched their heads off, put our fingers up their anuses and wiggled them about, fooling around, yelling loudly.

Li opened a thrush's gizzard with a sharp knife and, using his hands, emptied out its miserable contents, including small stones, for us to see. We stared at the dark brown insect heads, hard seeds, grass roots and bits of tree bark.

'They're eating horrible things,' Minami exclaimed.

'They're starving,' Li said.

'Everything outside the village is starving. Birds, beasts: they're all starving to death,' cried Minami. 'The people outside the village are reeling with hunger, and we're the only ones with full stomachs.'

We burst out laughing and Minami ran around in triumph brandishing the naked, gutted thrush. While we were outside the village, during our long mass evacuation, while we were moved around between temples, schools and farm outbuildings, we had usually been starving. Led by the warden, our comrades hurrying unswervingly to join our advance guard, fainting from hunger and pressing the flesh of their wasted stomachs, marching on the dark night road we had once passed along, and on the trolley track with the squeaking winch. We had to ensure the success of the village hunts to welcome them.

When all the birds were laid out on the snow with their hard spotty skins turning blue and black, leaking blood diluted with fat from their severed necks, they looked surprisingly scrawny and bony. But my brother's pheasant, with its stout fleshy thighs open and its yellow breast bones showing, looked grand. Piercing the small birds' legs with a thick wire, Li made a ring of meat and hung it over the fire. Then he ran the pheasant through from neck to anus with a sharpened oak branch and the boys, holding both ends of the branch, roasted the pheasant by turning it over and over.

Our younger comrades, yelling cheerfully, helped the soldier to slice vegetables into the pot and make a vast quantity of porridge, pouring in rice and water. My brother, wearing the pheasant's tail feathers shining like fire around his neck, took charge of passing the freshly washed vegetables to the soldier, but sometimes he ran up to gaze at his catch, roasting and dripping yellow-brown fat from all over its body, and sighed contentedly.

As the light of the setting sun sank over the snow in the heavy unstable time before moonrise, we began our luxurious feast. We surrounded the fire, munched the birds' flesh and soft bones, and ate the hot porridge. A sultry energy hung around our bodies as we noisily swallowed the food. Li brought out bottles of moonshine sake. The cloudy liquid was indescribably sour, and we all spat it out with a cry as soon as we took it in our mouths. The sake wouldn't go down our throats, but there was no need for it. Our blood was boiling with intoxication.

Li began to sing in his mother tongue and, quickly picking up that simple refrain which stuck firmly in our minds, we chorused his song.

'Is this the festival song?' I shouted over the others' singing.

'No, it's a funeral song,' Li shouted back, laughing and showing his quivering tongue. 'I learned it because my father died.'

'It's a festival song,' I declared, satisfied. 'Anything can be a festival song.'

We sang for a long time. Then suddenly the moon rose and the snow was bathed in a soft light. We all trembled, then ran yelling into the snow and danced wildly. After a short while we felt hungry again and went back to the cooking pot. There the soldier was on duty at the fire, hugging his knees with bowed head. We all thought he was stupid not to sing and dance.

Once we were full, drowsiness mingled with fatigue overtook us. Seeing off my brother and the others who went running back into the snow with Leo, I stayed by the fire, hugging my knees like the soldier. Li and Minami didn't try to leave the fire either. That meant the three of us were not exactly children any more.

'Even now, the war's still going on outside the village,' Minami said in a dreamy voice. 'If only there was no war, I'd be by the sea in the far south.'

'The war'll surely be over soon,' the soldier said, 'and it'll be the enemy's victory.'

We were silent. It was all the same to us. But the soldier, nettled by our indifference, stuck to his views.

'I ought to hide for just a short while, until the war's over.' The deserter's voice was hot and feverish, like a prayer. 'Once the country surrenders, I'll be free.'

'You're free now, aren't you? You can do anything you like in this village; wherever you lay your head, no one'll catch you.' I said. 'You're really free, aren't you?'

'We're still not free, you and I,' the soldier said. 'We're cut off.'

'Don't think about what's outside the village, don't say that,' I said angrily. 'We can do anything in this village. Don't speak about them outside.'

The soldier fell silent and we too quietened down.

Only the fire made a soft crackling noise. From outside, the voices of my brother and the others running around on the snow. I heard the dog barking.

'We're certain to be defeated in the war,' the soldier repeated after a short while, then suddenly lifted his head, and looking round at us, he asked:

'Well? You're silent, but don't you feel disgraced by defeat?'

'It's something they're doing, that the guys outside carrying guns who cut us off are doing,' I said calmly. 'What's it got to do with us?'

'You're scum, being so indifferent to your defeat,' the soldier said insistently.

'You're the one who ran away 'cos you were afraid of dying,' I said. 'And we're the scum?'

'We don't run away,' Minami finished him off, twisting his lips in a malicious smile. 'Worry about yourself.'

The soldier glared at us, burning with anger, then buried his forehead in his knees. I felt that he was squashed and humiliated, but I had no sympathy. There was a high wall between us and the soldier, and we couldn't climb over it. Despite his timidity, the soldier brought the outside world into the village and even now he was sticking with it. Those who are only half grown up, those who've become grown-ups, are incorrigible, I thought complacently.

'He said we're scum,' Minami said in a deeply satisfied voice and looked at us. We laughed loudly and the soldier didn't move, hanging his head.

When my brother and the others came running in, dusting

the snow off their clothes, we were almost asleep around the shrunken fire. They stood in front of us, their eyes shining with excitement. My drowsy head couldn't catch what they were saying all at once.

'What? Speak clearly,' the soldier said, half rising. 'Sick?'

'Yeah, she looks terribly sick,' my brother said earnestly. 'She's lying red-faced and groaning. She doesn't answer.'

I jumped up. I was choked with remorse that I had completely forgotten the girl in the warehouse.

'Did you go in and look?' I shouted, shaking my brother's shoulders and making the pheasant feathers glitter.

'When I went to say sorry about Leo,' he said, frightened, 'she just groaned.'

We ran out onto the snowy road that shone under the moon.

The fire on the warehouse floor had almost gone out. Walking on tiptoe, we surrounded the prostrate girl's body. Her face, floating up whitely, looked even more shrunken because of the fever. She was shivering rapidly and emitting unbelievably high-pitched gasps from her open mouth. I knelt on the earth floor and touched the writhing sinews in her neck with my finger. Contorting her lips and showing her gums, the girl twisted her neck violently and retreated from my finger. I was stunned, like a poleaxed goat on its back. The girl gave a long groan and mumbled a long-drawn-out word to herself. I gasped.

'You, light the fire,' the soldier said, pushing Minami's shoulder hard.

His voice suddenly had the gravity and calm of an elder. It wasn't the feeble, petty voice of the man who had gone on and on about the war. Minami, who had always sneered at him, obediently went out of the warehouse to get firewood without making a noise.

'You, find an ice bag and put snow and water in it,' the soldier said, looking straight at me.

'An ice bag?' I said despairingly. Where would something like that be?

'There's an ice bag,' Li panted, 'in the headman's house.'

'Go and get it,' the soldier said sternly, bending over the girl's head. 'And the others, stay by the fire in the school. If you make a racket, she'll die. Then her disease'll be transferred to you.'

The Korean boy and I ran out into the snow light and went up the hill.

'That deserter,' Li said, running breathlessly, 'studied a bit to be a doctor. He said so himself, though I didn't really believe him.'

I prayed hard that it was the truth. I too tried to believe it.

The headman's house was surrounded by a black-and-white chequered wall which darkly blocked out the moonlight. Li and I hesitated before the low gate and looked each other in the eye. The only proper house in the village, it flaunted moral order before us. We had exempted this house from our looting after the villagers' exodus. And now we understood the significance of that exemption clearly for the first time.

'If I break into this house, my mother'll be hounded by the villagers all her life. I'll be kicked out of the village,' Li said. 'I might be killed.'

My throat flushed in a brief spasm of anger, but a gentle encouraging moisture welled up softly in Li's eyes and spoke to me.

'You'll do it?' I said.

'Even if I get killed, I'll do it,' he said.

We climbed over the gate, ran quickly across the courtyard and broke open the wooden door with stones. The wide earth floor inside was even colder than outdoors and it smelt so mouldy that we could hardly breathe. When the little flame of the match in Li's hand ignited, the sulphur smoke stuffed up our nostrils. He moved the flame to the torch hanging on the black-painted pillar in the front porch. The interior was crammed with heavy furniture full of years. I looked around the seemingly immense earth floor and looked up at the splendid family altar on the high floor, beyond the tatami mats.

Li ran straight up there, opened the vermilion-lacquered door beneath the altar, showing his teeth in a smile as he pulled out a bulky paper bag, and jumped down. We climbed back over the gate.

'Every month me and my brother would sit on that earth floor for hours plaiting straw sandals. It was forced labour,' Li said as we ran. 'If we slacked, the old master would spit on me and my mother.'

He spat viciously himself. He was really excited by breaking into the headman's house, and his voice was shaking.

'We know where everything is in that house; ever since my father was a child, the people in that house made my family do everything for them. When I was repainting the privy, I'd crawl around in it all day covered in shit.'

'You were really brave,' I said, moved by a spirit of comradeship, then remembered the girl's words and was gripped by a sorrow so intense that it almost made me keel over in the snow and cry out loud. Biting my lips, I collected the snow for Li to put in the old-fashioned ice bag which he took out of the paper bag, and scooped up slushy water from the puddles of melted snow with both frozen hands.

'You're brave too,' he said, tying the mouth of the ice bag.

The soldier took the ice bag from us at the warehouse door. Then he urged us away, jerking his chin.

'She won't die, will she? She'll be saved?' I implored him.

'I don't know,' he said coldly. 'There's no medicine or anything; there's nothing I can do.'

Closing the door in our faces, he looked cold and detached, as though a layer inside his skin had begun to harden.

Li and I went back to the square in front of the school, pressing our shoulders together in silence. Fatigue swelled up inside me like a sponge soaking up water.

The comrades were sitting around the fire with sunken heads. I grew anxious when I saw my brother standing apart from their circle with his back turned defiantly towards them, hugging Leo. Minami stood up, took one step towards us and looked Li and me straight in the eyes. His lips were quivering. When he opened his mouth, swallowing spittle, I had an urge to restrain him. But it was too late.

'According to the soldier's diagnosis,' he said hastily, 'it looks like that girl's got the plague.'

Plague: that word. The word that immediately spread its leaves and roots wide all over the village, raging like a tempest, crushing everyone in its path, was shouted out from his throat, becoming a reality for the first time in that village where children had been left behind alone. I felt it agitate the boys sitting round the fire, causing a sudden panic.

'That's a lie,' I shouted. 'It's a lie.'

'I kept quiet until you came back,' Minami shouted. 'I swear the soldier told me so clearly. That girl dirties her bum with runny shit like blood. I saw it. She's got the plague.'

I saw the younger boys suddenly seized by fits of panic and I punched Minami's twitching throat hard. He fell down on the snow that had been melted by the fire and groaned, clutching his throat with both hands. Li held me back as I was about to kick his gut while he struggled for breath. Li's arm was brawny and hot. I stared at the comrades as they stood round the fire, trembling with sudden fright.

'It's not plague,' I said. But fear had soaked deep into them, and they wouldn't listen to me.

'Let's run for it, or we'll die as well,' a scared voice said. 'Go on, take us along, let's run for it.'

'I said it's not plague. Keep on whining, if you want to get punched,' I shouted, raising my voice to conceal the terror which had begun to infect me as well. 'There's no plague here.'

'I know,' another high-pitched voice said frantically. 'She caught the plague from the dog.'

I looked at my brother and Leo in astonishment. My brother turned his back on us, trying even harder to ignore the shouting, and pressed Leo's head against his chest.

'We know as well,' other boys said as if in unison. 'It's the fault of your brother's dog and you're concealing it.'

I was dazed, confronted for the first time by comrades who were against me.

'What's the dog done?' Li said in a sharp, terse voice. 'Eh? What's he done?'

'That dog dug up the bodies,' a tearful voice said weakly. 'Your brother buried them again. We saw him washing his hands and the dog's body. It's been ill ever since. And this morning it bit the girl's arm and gave her the disease. That's why the plague's broken out.'

The end of the boy's sentence dissolved into sobs. I was completely at a loss, and couldn't think about anything else but talking to my brother, who stubbornly kept his back to us.

'Hey, is it true about the dog? It's a lie, isn't it?'

Turning round into the comrades' gaze, my brother tried to move his lips, then looked down in silence. I groaned. The comrades surrounded him and the dog. Tucking his tail between his legs and pressing his shoulder against my brother's knee, the dog looked up at us.

'It's got the plague,' Minami said hoarsely. 'Though you tried to cover it up, we're sure that it gave the plague to the girl.'

'Everyone saw it bite her wrist,' said a comrade. 'Even though she wasn't doing anything, it bit her. It's mad'

'He's not mad,' my brother protested strongly. He was desperate to protect his dog. 'Leo hasn't got the plague.'

'What do you know; what do you really know about plague?' Minami said, persistently harassing him. 'It's your fault that the plague's broken out.'

My brother endured it all with his eyes wide open and his lips trembling. Then he yelled, clearly trying to suppress the anxiety which he was drawing back from.

'I don't know, but Leo hasn't got the plague.'

'Liar,' voices rebuked him. 'Everyone'll die because of your dog.'

Minami ran out of the circle of accusation and pulled up the green oak branch that the cooking pot was hanging from. Everyone was taken aback, and the circle widened.

'Stop it,' my brother shouted in terror. 'If you hit my Leo, I'll never forgive you.'

But Minami advanced implacably, and whistled sharply. Slipping through my brother's hands as he hastily bent down, the dog came forward, lured by the whistle. I saw my brother turn his imploring eyes towards me, but what could I do? The dog stood awkwardly, hanging out his tongue which looked even to me like a mass of fiercely multiplying germs.

'Li,' my brother shouted, but Li didn't move.

The oak branch came down, and the dog collapsed on the snow with a thud. We all looked at it in silence. Biting his lips, eyes full of tears, his body shaken by sobs, my brother started to stagger forward. But he couldn't look down at the twitching dog, whose black blood was gently soaking the fur over its ears. Shattered by rage and grief, he stirred and spoke.

'Who knew if Leo had the plague? Hey, all of you, who knew?'

He ran off sobbing, head down. Everyone gazed after his small shoulders that were shaking with sobs. I shouted to call him back, but he didn't return. I've betrayed my brother, I thought. How could I console my brother as he lay sobbing, burying his head in the dark granary's musty straw?

Perhaps I should have followed him and comforted him, hugging his shoulders. It might have been the best thing to do; but I had to stop the panic which had seized the younger boys and which might drive them into screaming hysteria. And I thought that now, while they were standing in shock with the poleaxed dog before them, was the best and probably the only opportunity left.

'You,' I shouted. 'Anyone who whines about plague, I'll smash their head in just like the dog. All right? I promise, the plague hasn't broken out.'

They fell silent, disheartened. They were obedient, cowed by the bloody oak bough in Minami's arms rather than my voice. Feeling I had succeeded, I repeated emphatically:

'All right, there's no plague or anything.'

Then I picked up my brother's necklace of pheasant feathers, covered with mud and snow, from where he had been sitting and put it in my coat pocket. Li and Minami threw the dog's carcass on the fire and piled wood on top of it. The weakened fire didn't burn up strongly and the dog's legs stuck out from the firewood for a long time.

'You lot,' I said to the younger comrades in a commanding tone, 'Go back and sleep. I'll hit anyone who makes a fuss.'

Minami looked at me with mocking eyes. That exasperated me.

'Minami, you go to bed too.'

'I won't take orders,' he said, showing hostility. He gripped the oak bough, which was smeared with the dog's hair and blood.

'You should go home,' Li said, eyeing Minami's oak bough. 'If you don't like it, you'll have me to deal with too.'

Minami twisted his face, pushed the oak bough into the fire and yelled at the comrades. 'Anyone who doesn't want to die alone like a dog, come 'n sleep with me. There's germs swarming all around those two.'

Li and I lingered by the fire, scorching our foreheads in the heat, and saw off the others, who had grown anxious and were running after Minami. At first there was the low dry sound of the flames. After that the fat melted and flowed, burning with a sizzling noise, sparks popped up, the thick smell of burning lumps of meat rose and stuck in the air around us. It wasn't the odour, lively and energetic, which had arisen when we roasted the pigeons, the shrikes and the pheasant, but the heavy taste of death. I bent over and vomited up some stubs of vegetables, rice grains, and hard tendons of bird meat. As I wiped my mouth with the back of my hand, Li gazed at me with eyes hollow with fatigue. Exhaustion flowed from them into my body like floodwater and jostled under my skin. I was so exhausted that I found it hard even to straighten up, and very sleepy. And I couldn't bear to stand in the smell of the burning dog any longer. I got up slowly, biting my lips, nodded to Li and turned my back on the fire. I wanted to sleep in the straw by my brother's side like a baby animal. My brother would forgive me, tired out as I was with a heart full of tears: these were sweet thoughts. The moon was hiding behind thick clouds and gave a pearly lustre to their distant rims. The snow had frozen again on the dark road and I felt it creaking under my soles. I went up the slope, the skin of my cheeks numb with cold.

The door of our granary was slightly ajar and the mat hanging behind it swung in the wind. I shouldered my way in and called to my brother. There was no reply. The fire on the earth floor was out and there was no smell of human beings. I took the box of matches from my trouser pocket and, bending over to block out the wind, lit a match. My brother's sleeping place was empty. Then I saw that his kit-bag was no longer on the grain bin and, in its place, the camel's-head-shaped tin-opener which I had lent him was standing there neatly with its handle pointing down. The household dust had settled during the short period in which we had made the granary our new home, and the place where my brother's kit-bag had lain was black and well-marked. The match flame burned my fingers. I screamed and threw it away, and dashed outside.

As I rushed down the slope I called my brother at the top of my voice. But the voice from my throat, held back by the cold and the dry air, resounded feebly in the darkness. Hey, hey, come back, where are you going, hey.

Leaning towards the fire and almost singeing his eyebrows, Li was poking the still unconsumed body of the dog with a stick. Its stomach had burst open and its brightly coloured entrails were about to burn up with a spitting noise. One end of the small intestine stood erect, trembling like a finger, then slowly swelled and reddened.

'Do you know where my brother is?' I said, my dry tongue sticking.

'Eh?' Li turned his blushing greasy face towards me. I was annoyed that he was so engrossed in the dog's incineration. 'Your brother?'

'He's not there; didn't he come to see the dog?'

'He's not there?' Li said, staring at the intestines as they burst with an obscene spluttering noise. 'I don't know.'

I sighed feverishly. 'Where the hell's he gone?'

'This really stinks. The blood's awfully slow to burn,' Li said. The stifling smell gushed out.

I ran up the narrow village road and went into the forest,

which pressed in on the sloping gravelled path from both sides, then came out on the stone pediment overlooking the valley that was the starting point for the closed-off trolley track. The valley was dark and only a loud noise of water arose. I shouted: hey, hey, come back, hey, don't go away, hey, hey.

No one answered. The birds and animals of the forest behind were also silent. They were hiding in the trees and grass, scared by the premonition of a fateful catastrophe which had attacked the village, pricking up their ears to listen to a human child's shouts. My shouts were absorbed by the deep ears of the creatures sitting in silence and never reached my runaway brother. Hey, hey, come back, hey, hey, don't go away, hey.

The light of a swinging lantern hanging on a man's arm appeared from the guard hut on the other side of the valley and moved a short distance. Then the sound of a blank warning shot rang round the valley. Burning with rage, I retraced the road through the forest and went back to the village. I've been abandoned by my brother, I thought. He didn't abandon me when I stabbed a senior student in the junior high school and was first sent to the reformatory; nor when I escaped and lived in squalor with a girl from the toy factory, and was then discovered by the police and my father and came home with dirty clothes and a nasty disease; nor when I was sent to the reformatory again. But now he had abandoned me.

I walked howling like a beast, shedding my tears on the snow. The dirty water coming in through my cracked soles soaked my chilblained toes and made them itch terribly, but I fiercely pushed my shoes into the ankle-deep snow and made no attempt to reach down and scratch them. If

I had bent down I couldn't possibly have straightened up and started walking again.

I stopped in front of the warehouse and listened hard. I could hear the girl's groans of agony from behind the dark, fiercely shut walls. I ran up and banged on the wooden door.

'Who is it?' the soldier's angry voice said.

'Is she going to get better?' I asked, choking with tears. 'She hasn't got the plague, has she?'

'It's you,' he said, after the sound of him getting up. 'I don't know if she'll get better. And I don't know if it's the plague.'

'If we show her to a doctor?' I said, but when I thought of the village doctor's vehement refusal of my plea, my courage failed. 'Ah, if only a doctor would come from somewhere.'

'Get some snow to put in the ice bag,' the tired and listless voice said from inside.

I knelt down in the snow and started to collect it with frozen, numbed fingers. My brother had abandoned me, and my first love was gasping with her small buttocks covered in excrement like blood. I felt the plague swamping the valley with terrible force like a cloudburst, catching me, overflowing all around us, leaving us unable to move. I was at a dead end, and all I could do was bend over in the dark night road and collect dirty snow, sobbing.

Chapter Nine:

The Return of the Villagers and the Slaughter of the Soldier

The plague spread during the night, showing its brutal strength, utterly defeating and overwhelming us abandoned children. The dawn was dark, and from morning on into broad daylight the village in the valley was dark, sealed in with a dirty fog. The sun penetrating the thick layer of semi-transparent air melted the filthy snow, which turned into a slushy bog. Our lethargy and despair, the swarming germs, the gigantic host of minute germs that were going to drive us into unconsciousness, into fits of gibberish that would burn our throats like fire, were seething like pale yellow gelatin boiled down from cattle bones and hide, swamping the liquefied village.

My comrades stayed deep inside their houses and didn't venture out. Li also shut himself up in his small house that smelt of pigs. I lay down on the granary floor with my eyes shut and from time to time wiped away the cold sweat that kept on soaking my underwear. None of us had yet contracted the plague, but since it would attack furiously without warning like a blow from a strong arm, we waited for it inside the dark houses. And only the soldier, who — despite lack of sleep — directed our anxious vigil with such authority that even Minami complied, fought the plague which had caught the girl first. Some boys ran out of the houses in their desperate anxiety and banged on the closed warehouse door; the soldier's jeering voice arose, and that sent the panic-stricken boys back home again. Sobs and shouts of rage resounded emptily everywhere in the village.

I lay down in the darkness, staring upwards, and sweated it out. The girl's smooth dry sex, like a summer flower, her arse soiled with excrement, her face, small and red from the fever, appeared and vanished rapidly before me. That image came and went, and every so often gave me a shameful erection. I sometimes thought I heard the sound of my brother's soft footsteps and became obsessed with it, trying to believe it. I always felt my brother standing beyond the stagnant air, my brother rubbing at the dry mist and dust with his hands, but, smiling shyly, he came no nearer.

In the evening I saw the soldier going towards the common grave down in the valley's soft earth and underbrush, carrying a small object wrapped in a rug, and some of my comrades followed him a couple of metres behind. I ran up and joined them, and sobbed as I watched the soldier doggedly dig up the earth then bury the lump wrapped in the rug, occasionally casting stern glances which kept us at a distance.

After that, he went up the slope, leaning forward, and

returned to the warehouse, where he silently began to pile up branches and firewood on the floor. This time we helped him, also in silence. After watching the small warehouse belch fire and smoke then burn up in an enormous tower of flames, we scattered and went back to our dark houses. The soldier had ordered us back.

Hugging my knees, I sat on the storehouse's earth floor where the fire had already gone out and sobbed for a long time. My head hurt as if it was being squeezed. Then I went out onto the dark road and called my brother. He didn't appear with his shy smile. I went down the slope.

The deserter was standing in front of the razed warehouse, in the slush melted by the heat of the flames. He was sobbing with his head down and his shoulders shaking. I went up to him. We looked at each other in the darkness. The deserter kept silent and didn't open his mouth. And I had no words to say to him. I wanted to tell him that I had been abandoned by my brother and my lover. But I just fretted like an infant who didn't know the words, tears in my eyes.

Giving up, I shook my head, turned my back on the deserter and went up the road to the granary. The snow was freezing up once more and had begun to harden. Suddenly the soldier came chasing after me along the dark road. He put his arm round my shoulder. With nothing to talk about, we went back to the granary and lay down on the boards, our bodies entwined. I thought now that the soldier's weak stubbly jaw and pale bony cheeks looked heroic and beautiful. As I started to sob, he drew my head to his chest that smelt of sweat, and he was entirely gentle with me. Then, for a short while, though we were exposed to the menace of the plague, exhausted, so pathetically despairing that we could hardly get a word out of our mouths, we tasted a small miserable pleasure in each other. Silently we bared our poor goose-pimpled buttocks, losing ourselves in the motion of cunning fingers.

I awoke before dawn from a shallow sleep, hearing a stifled cry and, trembling with cold, I found that the soldier was no longer in my arms. It was dawn. I thought I heard a low voice calling me again. My brother's mild friendly smile, his teeth gleaming between slightly parted lips. I jumped up and looked out the window, rubbing the fine ice droplets on the glass with my fingers. Beyond the thick layer of milk-white fog there was a faint rosy light which gradually expanded.

Then suddenly, at the moment that the birdsong stopped like the abrupt cessation of a tempest, several dark stolid men, villagers with sharply pointed bamboo spears and the stiff expressionless faces of beasts, were silently standing there in the current of mist and staring at me. We stared at each other for a short while as if looking at rare animals through the glass window, which at once froze up whitely. I was stunned and gasped with surprise, then I felt a great relief welling up like warm water. The villagers had returned.

Behind the men, a short individual with a strong jaw stuck his head out from beyond the current of mist and peered in at me and behind me. It's the blacksmith, I realized, and I even felt nostalgia when he shouldered his way through the wooden door he had opened, holding a short iron bar poised like a weapon. But he quickly looked me up and down, with his thick, tight-shut lips and stern expression, and turned his eyes towards mine more like a man looking at a beast than one looking at a fellow human being. He's checking to see if I'm concealing a weapon, I thought, senselessly perturbed by my vulnerability.

'It's no good resisting,' said the blacksmith who had sprung up nimbly, grabbing my arm. 'Come with us.'

I was being treated like a prisoner of war. But with my arms grasped by the blacksmith's huge, firm, gauntletted hands, I had no intention of resisting. The grown-ups have come back; we'll be saved from the threat of the plague; at last the villagers have come back. . .

'Come with us quietly,' said the blacksmith. 'Or I'll hit you.'

'I'll come with you,' I said hoarsely. 'I want to bring my things along. I won't resist.'

'That?' The blacksmith pointed with his iron bar at my kit-bag on the grain bin sunk in the darkness. 'Get it.'

I pushed the camel's-head tin-opener that my brother had left behind into my kit-bag and wound the bag's cord around my upper arm. The blacksmith waited while I did so, scrutinizing me with suspicious eyes. I thought that a new myth of our reformatory boys' brutality had percolated to the furthest reaches of the mountain villages.

When I went out into the gusting fog and wind side by side with the blacksmith, who was pushing his shoulder against me, the men surrounded us. We went down the slope in silence. The blacksmith pulled me up violently by my shoulder as I slipped in the snow and wouldn't let go of my thin muscles.

'I won't run away,' I said, but his fingers, more and more resolute, made my shoulder muscles ache. The men walked the short distance they had to drag me over, and the blacksmith kept his hold on my shoulder. The men's bamboo spears noisily dug into the snow frozen by the cold dawn air.

My comrades emerged from the mist, gathered around the dead bonfire in front of the school, holding their kit-bags or laying them on their knees. They greeted me with a cheer. Running my eyes quickly over them, I searched among them for my brother. But by the time I joined them, pushed in amongst them by the blacksmith, and squatted down in the mist by the bonfire that smelt of coal, my small hope had been betrayed. And as I watched other boys being brought in one by one in the mist, my hope of seeing the gentle motion of my brother's shoulders and his handsome head kept on being betrayed.

But I didn't shake off a slight rush of excitement. And the boys around me, suddenly released from their fear of the plague, sopped up a cheerful, frenzied elation. The villagers have come back, we thought. Little by little we began to believe sincerely that the plague had only been able to snatch the girl away from us like the last flower and then had rapidly abated. And that planted joy in our group. Some of us, poking each other and making obscene gestures, even laughed.

Minami came up, laughing incessantly in an excited voice, with one of the villagers holding onto his arm. He joined us with his cheeks red and glowing, eyes shining and laughter blowing like small bubbles from his wet lips.

'He came to haul me off when I was doing my morning make-up squatting on the floor,' he shouted. 'And he was fascinated by my bare bum; he hit me 'cos it stank. Crazy, isn't it? It was in the middle of my morning make-up.'

'Morning make-up?' a younger comrade asked innocently, released from his anxiety, inflating Minami's pride.

'I mean morning make-up for my bum.'

The boys around him laughed childishly and he triumphantly demonstrated his obscene posture. Everyone was light-hearted, as if waiting for the roll call before setting off on some excursion.

The fog lifted and the low cloudy sky appeared, brimming with wet morning light, melting the dirty snow that had frozen up again mixed with mud. All of our comrades had been brought in from their temporary homes. The villagers surrounded us with stiff expressionless faces, clutching bamboo spears and hunting rifles. Compared to their silence, my comrades' frenzied excitement seemed to rise up unnaturally. When the fog at last cleared away entirely, we saw a constable from the police post and the village headman coming forward, pushing the taciturn villagers aside. The tension developed a vague focus and gelled around us.

'You've really fucked about,' the headman shouted, his anger erupting, 'Breaking into other people's homes, stealing food, burning down the warehouse; what kind of vermin are you?'

We swayed in shock. Our frenzied joy immediately degenerated into dark foreboding.

'We'll report everything you've done to the authorities, you delinquents, you good-for-nothings.'

'Who burned down the warehouse?' the constable demanded in a snarling voice. 'Come on, tell us the truth.'

Minami shrugged his shoulders defiantly and tried to sit down, placing his kit-bag on the snow. Immediately the constable jumped on him, pulled him up by his shirt front and punched him on the jaw.

'Hey, it's you, isn't it? You're the arsonist,' he shouted in a voice full of hatred, prodding Minami. 'Come on, spit it out, you bastard, fooling around with us. You started the fire, didn't you.'

'It wasn't me,' Minami cried, squirming in pain. 'It wasn't me; it was the soldier who ran away from the cadets who did it.'

The constable loosened his hold and looked at him, and there was consternation amongst the villagers. We all looked at Minami reproachfully.

'The deserter was here, was he? Well, where's he hiding?'

'I don't know,' Minami said.

'You bastard,' the constable groaned, knocking him down and kicking him in the chest. 'Don't fool around with us.'

'Where's the soldier? Come on, confess,' the headman said, twisting a comrade's arm. 'You're really degenerate. Come on, where's the soldier?'

The young boy spoke, prompted by pain, anger and, above all, fear. 'He ran off into the mountains. I don't know anything else.'

'Lock them up,' the constable shouted. 'Then reassemble.'

The others hurried us away. We walked with feet suddenly grown heavy, remembering our hunger, our anxiety redoubled, hearing the villagers gathering behind us. Then we were shut up in a small outhouse attached to the school building, so nervous that there were tears in our eyes, angry and despairing. Outside a bolt was roughly pushed into place.

The constable's orders and a wave of running footsteps with the clash of bamboo spears rose up. It's the hunt, I thought. They're going to hunt down the soldier and catch him. He noticed the villagers returning before I did and escaped. But they'll soon catch up with him because he's tired from lack of sleep after tending the girl.

'That lot,' Minami explained to those around him, feigning cheerfulness to divert attention from his slip-up, 'They've come back to scout around and see if we're all dead or not. The women and children still haven't come back yet, have they? They're confused because we're still alive. What's more, there was someone like me doing his morning make-up.'

And he laughed lewdly. But the cheerful frenzied excitement of earlier on had left the others, and Minami's unnaturally high-pitched laughter sank and was absorbed into the reawakening of deep, clammy anxiety which held its usual heaviness, and the return of our sense of fretful anticipation, and triggered no wave of reaction. In the end, he squatted down in morose silence, chewing his nails. We waited like that for a long time.

Even when a boy who desperately needed to urinate banged on the door and pleaded, there was no response from outside. He had to do it in a corner of the shed, pale with humiliation and shame. The small shed immediately filled with the pungent smell of urine.

Some boys peered out through the gaps between the weatherboards and told the others of their small discoveries. At first there was no movement outside. But towards noon the comrades who were pressing their noses against the boards on the side that overlooked the valley's common grave made a great discovery. Everyone heard a strange wordless growling and peeped out through the boards, piling up on each other's backs or lying flat on the floor between each other's legs. A common anger spread from body to body, extricating us one by one from the state of individual panic, yoking us firmly together.

Five of the villagers were working in the valley's communal grave, swinging their hoes, their backs and shoulders bathed in the pale sunlight, their downcast faces thrown into shadow. And they dug up the corpses which we had devotedly buried like precious bulbs and lay them down in the meadow where the snow still lay. We couldn't tell which of them was our ex-comrade or the girl's fresh corpse that had become the first bud of our fear. They were all covered in mud; just a blue and earth-coloured mess. But when the villagers had laid firewood in the gutted grave and small sharp flames from the burning of the dead piled on top started to stir up the stagnant afternoon air, our anger became explicit. Even Minami shed tears, biting his lip. It was a kind of ritual to compel us to acknowledge that every being in the village, including corpses, even corpses that had been buried, was back under the control of the adults. The grown-ups did it half-heartedly, rather bored, and little by little other figures appeared on the valley slope. The returning village women and children watched impassively.

We had possessed and controlled the village, I thought, suddenly smitten by trembling. We had not been cut off in the village, we had occupied it. We had yielded up our dominion to the grown-ups without resistance, and in the end we were shut up in the shed. We'd been fooled, really fooled.

I lifted my cheeks from the boards and went back to the opposite corner. Minami turned round with sharp narrowed eyes reddened by tears and spoke to me.

'They're really fucking about.'

'Yeah,' I said. 'They're really fucking about.'

It was us who had looked after the empty village for the last five days; we even had the festival for the hunt; and they shut us up. They're really fucking about.

'I wonder what Li's doing,' one of the comrades said. 'Will he get caught as well?'

'If only he'd come and get us out of here,' Minami shouted in mounting anger. 'And if only we had guns, we'd drive off the peasants, the dirty bastards.'

I felt a warm comradeship for Minami welling up. If I had a gun, I'd shoot everyone down and make their blood flow. But Li didn't come to rescue us. And we didn't have any guns either. I sat leaning against the boards, hugging my knees, and closed my eyes. Then Minami came and sat next to me, nudging me with his shoulder. He whispered to me in a low, hot voice.

'I'm sorry about the business with your brother.'

But I wanted to avoid thinking about my brother.

'Your brother's nimble and fast on his feet,' Minami said. 'Perhaps he hid in the grass and watched us get caught. I'm really sorry.'

Suddenly we heard two shots with a short interval between them, probably warning shots, deep in the forest behind us. We immediately stood up and listened. But there were no more shots. A fresh shiver of anxiety filled us. We waited until the air in the shed had grown really dark and our faces had become just white blurs.

Then we heard the sudden barking of hunting dogs, angry swearing, confused footsteps, and the adult villagers coming down from the forest. We pressed our eyes against the thin strips of golden light shining through the boards. The villagers were surrounding the quarry of their cruel chase.

They walked quite slowly and calmly. Only when the children tried to join in their procession did rough voices start to jump around amongst them. They came walking up with their guns and spears held vertically against their sides and their heads down. Then the deserter came walking up hesitantly, his shoulders shaking, as if he was impeded by the glowing, lustrous evening air, the wind smelling faintly of snow and leaves. He had now been stripped of his jacket and was wearing just a shirt of rough cloth with the sleeves rolled up as though it was the middle of summer. When the procession surrounding him passed by in front of the shed, we saw that the dirt on his small pinched face had dried to the colour of clay; that the brown cloth which covered his belly, reproducing an unnaturally elastic motion above the unsteady support of his hips, was torn; that the tear was stained dark brown; and that a soft, fresh, watery thing, a thing that caught the dim light and made slippery, vividly coloured pulsations, was dangling from it. Each time it wobbled with his step it gleamed in the dim golden light.

The soldier tripped as he stepped onto the road leading down the slope from the square in front of the school and tried to stop himself falling over, clumsily swinging his long arms. It was a pitiful and childish gesture, and made us weep. But two sturdy villagers promptly grabbed his shoulders and went on marching, almost dragging him. As the procession went out of sight, women, old people and children wearing clothes wadded with cotton up to their necks came hurrying after it like a fresh strong wind after a storm.

We took our eyes from the boards, sat down on the earth floor and stared at our feet in silence. Our legs, dried and white with the skin peeling off like fish scales, our small scrawny feet like those of birds, smelly and covered in dirt, our canvas shoes, filthy and full of holes that covered them, and the ostentatious symbol which showed the reformatory's location. We stayed that way for a long time, looking down in silence, crying and scared. One of the boys stood up and urinated against a corner of the weatherboarding, his hips trembling from his sobs, and sprayed hot yellow urine all over the place.

We heard a restless metallic sound of swords banging against each other and regular energetic footsteps coming nearer. We put our foreheads to the boards once more and saw two military policemen, the headman and the constable pass hastily through the bluish twilight air that had already lost its shine. None of them paid any attention to the shed where we were interned, and they sank from sight down the slope. We slumped down again, heads lowered, and relaxed our vigilance towards the outside.

'The villagers came back unwillingly,' Minami said, 'because the MPs came to catch him.'

'I wonder what'll happen to that soldier,' asked a voice gummed up with the traces of tears. 'I guess he'll probably be killed.'

'Killed?' said Minami, sneering. 'You saw the soldier's guts sticking out, didn't you? Do you think that someone who's been stabbed in the gut by bamboo spears will last for long, as he waits for them to kill him?'

'It must really hurt to walk with your guts hanging out,' the boy said, sobbing once more. 'It must hurt to be stabbed with bamboo spears.'

'Stop blubbering,' Minami said, hitting the weeping boy's quivering side and making him groan. 'All right? You'll get stabbed *there* by the village lunatics.'

The guts peeping out from the soldier's belly quietly swelled up and filled our heads that were heavy with fatigue and invading drowsiness. They affected us like a poison. Some occasionally burst into tears in the silence and others wet themselves where they sat, making transparent puddles round their arses and feet. I thought I should tear myself loose from the deep intense fear which was engulfing my comrades. And I thought I should dig up and focus on the traces of the hunger inside me which hadn't reached me even though it must certainly be gnawing at me. But I felt neither hunger nor cold; nothing moved inside me apart from the nausea rising to my throat and my burning mouth.

'I'm hungry,' I said hoarsely, but the end of the sentence faded away and I had to repeat it several times in order to make my comrades understand. 'I'm hungry.'

'Uh?' Minami looked at me, his eyes childish with surprise. 'You're hungry?'

'I feel sort of hungry,' I said slowly, and I felt the words starting to induce sensation in my intestines like a magic spell. That spread to Minami first and then, swiftly, to the others.

'I'm really hungry too,' Minami said excitedly. 'Dammit, if only there was some bird meat left.'

My spell had taken effect. A few minutes later we were desperate boys shut up in a small shed and suffering from starvation. I myself was almost reeling with starvation. And we hungered desperately without expecting that the wooden door would open and food be brought in by the ferocious villagers.

But after a while the door was suddenly opened from outside, and what was thrust in roughly through the narrow opening was not food but Li, completely covered with mud, blood and nameless filth. Stung by surprise, we looked up at him as he stood in the dark shed, his lips trembling with anger, but since we were suffering so badly from self-induced hunger no one stood up or said anything.

Li looked around at us, standing and frowning, narrowing his eyes even more, then came and sat down so close to me that our sides almost touched. A stifling smell of fresh blood and tree buds rose from his body. There were countless scratches, with dried blood sticking to them, from his strong neck to his cheeks and around his ears, and his eyes held a burning force in their depths like those of a forest animal. The sum of many hours' worth of danger spent hiding in the forest and fleeing through the shrubs was powerfully brought home to me. And I was consoled by the fact that he was injured, covered with dried blood and, even more, nearly euphoric with anger.

'I thought you'd got clean away,' I said to Li, whose lips were twitching in silence. 'It was bad luck.'

'Bad luck?' he said. 'I'm pissed off.'

'You're not the only one,' Minami said.

Li looked at him, then looked at me, and hesitated. He tried to overcome his hesitation. The smooth skin of his face suddenly swelled and bulged. He obviously wanted to speak to me.

'Hey, what is it?' I said.

'I went down the valley,' he answered in a rush, 'because I thought I'd have a hard time when the villagers came back. I left everything behind and went down the valley. I was going to get away along the riverbank. I tied a rope around a trolley support and went down.'

'This morning?' Minami said. 'I'd have come with you if you'd woken me.'

'As I walked between the rocks in the valley,' Li said in one breath, staring at me, ignoring Minami's comment, 'I found your brother's kit-bag. I found your brother's bag tangled up with bits of wood and dead cats where the water level had fallen as the flood went down, then I. . .'

I grabbed his shoulders as he broke off and shook him. I felt as though a big dark pit had opened in my head and the whole of me was about to tip straight into it. I couldn't make a sound.

'I. . .' Li writhed, squeezed tight by my trembling fingers, and implored me with his eyes. 'After I'd picked it out with a stick, I came back through the forest to give it to you.'

I was overwhelmed by sudden sobs, fits of sobbing which swelled up hugely inside and burned my chest and throat, and I let go of his shoulder and cried aloud, pressing my forehead against the boards.

'What did you do with the bag?' Minami asked, lowering his voice to avoid an eruption of my sorrow. 'Well? Did you bring it? Why didn't you bring it to him?'

'Because I was found in the forest and chased by the villagers,' Li said, puzzled. 'I threw it into some bushes because I didn't want them to think I'd stolen it. After that, other villagers with bamboo spears were suddenly standing in my way, so there was no escape.'

'You'll take us to where you threw it away, won't you?' Minami said at once. 'If it's not there, I'll make you sorry. It was a memento of his brother.'

Turning round quickly, I made a grab for Minami and saw that his eyes, sharp like a bird's, were filled with tears. The anger and muscular tension melted from my body and sorrow spread in its wake. I shook my head, holding my knees, then buried my forehead in them and groaned.

Late at night, after a long time had passed, a cry of pain suddenly arose in the distance and was immediately stifled, though a brief echo reverberated round the valley. My comrades rose from their cramped sleeping positions and searched each other's fear-wracked eyes.

'There was a military police car on the other side of the valley,' Li said. 'They want to take him away with them before he dies. They must be tying him on the trolley and sending him across to the other side.

'With his guts hanging out,' Minami said, 'doing that is the same as killing him.'

'They kill each other,' Li said, filled with hatred. 'We hid him, but the Japanese kill each other. The MPs, the constables and the peasants with their bamboo spears; a load of people hunt down those who've got away into the mountains and stab them to death. I don't understand what they do.'

Once more the desperate scream arose as if coming from a throat about to expire with agony, and its echoes resounded clearly across the valley for a short while, then it was soon stifled and died away. And that piercing voice bounced off our clotted expectations and reached our ears no more. I saw that Li, who was quietly pricking up his ears, had clear dark eyes, truly the eyes of a Korean. He looked back at my eyes, where the tears had begun to dry.

Then a great many confused footsteps came back to the square in front of the school, and it was only a short time before the heavy sound of the beams which held the shed's wooden door being removed rang out. The villagers were holding thick sheaves of torches, and in that bright, flickering, thickly-coloured light the headman came into the shed first. Then a lot of villagers followed after him and immediately filled the shed. We were pushed into the corner, into the stink of our own urine.

Chapter Ten:
Trial and Banishment

The youngest boy suddenly sobbed and sat down in terror, sticking out his chin. We and the villagers watched stale-smelling urine spread quickly over the earth floor from between his knees. And we all knew the cause of his sudden terror. A reddish-brown gooey substance was stuck to the freshly cut tip of the bamboo spear held in the right hand of the tall thin man immediately behind the headman, and what was clearly part of a human intestine was lodged in the spear's hollow bore. Our eyes were drawn to it. And the nausea was hard to bear. Some of the comrades bent over to vomit and choked cries arose. The villagers stared at them in silence.

'Is everybody here?' the headman asked, turning after running his stern eyes over us.

No one replied. The shed was filled only with silence and groans of vomiting that thickened the air.

'How many have run away?' the headman asked again.

'Two are missing since they came to the village,' said a man whose spear was scraping against a low crossbeam, 'but one died before *that*, so it's just one.'

When he said 'before *that*', he lowered his voice, stressing the vowels. That showed that the villagers had begun to convince themselves that the 'incident' was already over and had become a legend, a fable of a past natural disaster. But right now we were trying to live the 'incident' in the present. We would be dragged into it, our feet entangled, and would have to go on struggling.

'We dug up and burned the corpses they buried,' said the other man, 'but the other child's body was only the village girl. He's probably run off into the mountains.'

'Hey, you lot,' the headman said, thrusting himself forward, 'where's he hiding? If you keep quiet, we'll set the dogs loose. When they find him, his head'll be bitten off. How's that?'

I looked down, biting my lip. Anger quickly plunged me into reawakening sorrow, and the sorrow mingled with the anger and intensified. Li's big bony hand hesitantly stroked my thigh. That consoled me, but my eyeballs were wrapped in a film of bitter tears and I couldn't see his fingers.

'You know about it, don't you?' said the headman to a younger boy, whose lips were quivering with fear.

'I don't know,' he replied, gasping. 'He wasn't with us yesterday. I really don't know.'

'You filthy reformatory brats,' the headman shouted, suddenly enraged. 'You never come straight out with anything. Are you trying to fool with us? We can wring your scrawny necks at one go; we can even beat you to death.'

We certainly didn't mean to fool with the villagers. We

were sweating with terror from our bellies and armpits. Whenever the man who was gripping the bamboo spear smeared with blood and fat moved or shuffled his feet, our palpitations rose, then subsided.

'You deserve to be beaten to death for any one of the things you did while we were away,' the headman berated us, showing jagged teeth that glittered brutally with moisture. 'You broke into the houses and stole food. What's more, you slept in them and left piss and shit all over the place. Someone broke the tools. And to cap it all, you set fire to the warehouse.'

He stepped forward and cuffed the frightened cheeks of all those within reach with the backs of his hard thick-skinned hands, which became soaked with children's' tears of anger, fear and humiliation.

'Who was it? Hey, which one of you messed up the altar in my house. Hey, you sons of whores, you sons of bitches, who was it?'

I was terrified whenever the headman's brawny thighs came close to me, but I looked up and endured the scrutiny of the villagers behind him. Their eyes were full of rage and their open mouths, dribbling tension-induced saliva, accused us bitterly. Who was it who stole my food? Who lit a fire on my house's earth floor? Who did obscene scrawls on the walls of my house and the living-room ceiling?

'Do you realize, we've been thinking about your punishment for a long time. You brats. Do you realize what we're going to do with you, you lot that never come straight out with anything.'

One of the boys prodded on the shoulder by the head-man stood up. He was shaking.

'I haven't done anything,' he said feebly. 'Please forgive me.'

When he had been knocked to the floor with one blow, the next lamb to be singled out stood up and repeated the spineless excuse.

'Forgive me. It was because we didn't know what to do.'

My comrades stood up and pleaded one by one, then were knocked down and kicked. But no one resisted. We were beaten and submissive, and the headman rampaged and shouted on his own for a long time.

Then he suddenly stopped bellowing, halted the movement of his flailing arms and put his hands on his hips. He stared at us, shook his head, and went out, pushing the villagers aside. We stiffened. The villagers also stood stiffly and seemed to await his return. Then several of them went out, summoned from outside, and after that, when a bunch of new faces appeared in the narrow doorway, Li shrank down even more. The new faces had oddly paler, smoother skin than the villagers. They turned their vague, passive eyes towards us and made no accusations.

'Are they your mates?' I said, right next to Li's ear, but he didn't reply.

I saw that blood had congealed and stuck together and made a clot in his ear. Then a long silence, and within it the sound of pure, warm saliva lodged in young throats being swallowed and the villagers' ponderous movements. That transmitted heavy waves to the people gathered close-packed outside the shed, who kept on patiently trying to peer inside.

Tired and wracked by sleepiness, we stayed still, ringed by the villagers' scrutiny. We waited for a long time.

After an eternity the headman and the others came back again. We looked up and saw that the feverish rage had left the headman's eyes and mouth.

'You lot, have you thought carefully?' he said. 'Have you thought about the horrible things you did?'

After he had looked us over while we kept silent, he spoke carefully in a low cunning voice, almost whispering. 'We can't do anything more about what you did. We'll let it go.'

A relief tacky with a strange unpleasantness, a callow relief that lingered with an unnatural aftertaste, tried to insinuate itself into us. After that came astonishment. We were completely dumbfounded. One of my comrades, whimpering nervously, started crying with relief. What was more, he firmly lifted his small chin, wrinkling the space between his dirty narrow eyebrows, and even tried to smile.

'Tomorrow morning, the warden from your reformatory will arrive bringing the rest of the boys; then your evacuation period will begin officially,' the headman said in a mild voice, turning his hard eyes on us. 'We won't report your crimes to the warden. Instead of that, we've something to tell you as well. We'll say you've been leading normal lives since you arrived in this village. There was no plague in the village. The villagers didn't take flight. We'll do something like that. That way, it's less trouble. Understand?'

In my mind a half-opened lid suddenly slammed shut. That spread to the bodies around me and all my comrades resumed their staunchly defiant stance towards the headman, their correct posture. We were going to be duped. And nothing could be more humiliating, more dumb and ignoble, than being 'duped'. That would make even the most miserable shabby faggot blush all over with shame.

'All right, say it.' When the headman spoke, looking round us, his fake calm shaken by our indifference, we comrades regained our proper attitude, reforged the firm ties between fellows and stuck our chests out provocatively towards him, our eyes shining.

'Hey, you, you'll say it, won't you?' the headman said, jabbing at Minami with his finger.

'I'm not gonna do that kind of thing,' Minami said, sneering openly. 'We got cut off, just us, abandoned and left in the middle of the plague. It's true, isn't it?'

'That's right. You abandoned us,' another comrade said. Then everyone around him shouted together, chiming in.

'Stop that lying.'

Thrown off balance by our counterattack, the headman immediately became furiously angry and let his rage overflow. He flailed his arms and sprayed saliva around, showing the blackened gold-capped teeth in his open mouth.

'If you lot fool with us, we won't let you off. Do what I say, or we'll beat you to death. We've loads of strong men who can easily turn the screws on you. Don't you know that?'·

To keep my comrades from rebounding into terror, I had to shout against the headman. I stood up with my head reeling anaemically from fear of him and the brutish men behind him, but I opened my mouth wide and shouted.

'We won't be conned. We won't be duped and deceived by you. *You* shouldn't fool with us.'

The headman opened his mouth, glaring at me, and tried to say something, but I wasn't going to accept that. I had to go on shouting for as long as possible before he started to speak.

'We were abandoned by your village. Then we lived in the village where there might have been an outbreak of plague. Then you came back and locked us up. I'm not going to keep quiet about it. I'll tell everything that was done to us and everything that we saw. You stabbed the soldier to death. I'll tell his family about it. You sent me back when I went to beg you to come and examine us. I'm going to tell all of it. I'm not going to keep quiet.'

The thick haft of a villager's spear struck me a glancing blow on the chest, and I fell, hitting my head against the boards, and groaned. I couldn't catch my breath. And the bitter taste of blood in my mouth, then gushing out of my nose. I lifted my face, moaning, and dragged myself to the corner of the weatherboarding to avoid the next attack. The blood flowed from my nose and smeared the skin under my ears, on my neck and under my shirt. My nose stopped bleeding almost immediately since I was used to being beaten, but the fear that crept from my abdomen up my back and the tears that spread over a sticky membrane on which the blood had started to coagulate wouldn't stop.

'All right? If you lot don't want to end up like that, do as you're told,' the headman said after a moment, slowly and menacingly. 'Admit that nothing happened here and that you saw nothing. Then from tomorrow you can start your evacuation properly.'

The boys shrank down as much as they could and kept quiet in the dim light, like small animals. They kept as quiet as they possibly could, and that was conveyed to me. And I knew that it couldn't go on for long.

'Any one of you who's against the village's ideas, sit down like that,' the headman said. 'Those who are going to go along with the village's version, stand up and go over to the wall. We'll give you rice balls.'

A small bud of agitation sprouted and rapidly grew. The man who held the bloodstained bamboo spear stepped forward and shouted in a hoarse voice.

'Anyone who objects to what the headman says, sit there, and I'll smack you one.'

A boy jumped up and walked over to the wall, breathing heavily, and sobbed with his forehead leaning against the boards, his body shaking. Then other comrades stood up slowly and followed him, chests burning with shame. After a short while there was only Minami and Li, trembling with his head bowed, left on my side.

'Hey, you're still holding out?' the headman rebuked us sternly, and the villager's bamboo spear prodded Minami's cheek. 'That's enough. Say that you saw nothing and that you weren't abandoned.'

Blood trickled slowly from the corner of Minami's cut lip, and cold indifferent scorn filled and distorted his pale face. He stood up, avoiding the bamboo spear once more aimed at his face. He obstinately turned away from me, and spoke as he went over to the comrades' side.

'I saw it; I had a pretty good time being abandoned; it's easy to keep quiet about it.' And he bawled violently at the backs of the boys around him, who were looking down and shivering. 'Hey, you're hungry, aren't you? You want to eat rice balls.'

'Li.' The triumphant headman's voice dominated the shed. 'Are you defying me?'

Li looked up at him, timidly moving his head just a little, and stuttered haltingly as if pleading with him.

'I. . .' He used a fairly servile tone of voice. 'I was going to stay in the village and guard it, staying here with the others. At first I thought of running away, but later I thought I'd rather guard the village. We even had the hunting festival.'

'What about it?' the headman interrupted. 'Eh? What's that got to do with it.'

'Then. . .I. . .'

'If you disobey me,' the headman said callously, without listening to him, 'have you thought what'll happen to your settlement? We can kick you out any time, even tomorrow.'

Li stuck it out. I saw the smooth pale faces among those piled up in the dark doorway grow agitated and disturbed. But they said nothing.

'The constable said that the deserter might have been hiding in the Korean settlement. If that's so, then everyone in the settlement will be thrown in jail. You won't be able to come back without our help. Don't you understand?'

Li took his hand away from my knee. Then suddenly he stood up and went outside, passing through the villagers with his head bowed, making a sobbing noise in his throat. Seized by rage and sorrow, I watched the people from his settlement run outside and the faces of other villagers come piling in after them.

Now I was the only one left. The headman slowly turned back to meet my fierce gaze. We stared at each other in silence.

'Hey, how about you?' the headman said. 'Are you going to stick by yourself over such a trivial point? It really doesn't matter. All it was, was that the villagers were away for a few days. It was you who did bad things during that time. But we've said we'll let that go.'

I kept sullenly silent. The villagers' eyes bored into me. The village women brought in rice balls piled up on big plates and soup in an iron cooking pot. Then my comrades were given rice balls and bowlfuls of hot soup and started eating. It was certainly real food, the wholesome humane meal which we were never able to get during our long spell in the reformatory, during our evacuation marches and during our time as children on our own. It was rice rolled by the hands of village women who lived free in the fields, meadows and streets, and soup which had been tasted by the tongues of ordinary housewives, not the cold mechanical meals cut off from affection and ordinary life. My comrades mulishly turned their backs on me as they devoured it, clearly feeling shame towards me. But I myself was ashamed of the saliva flowing in my mouth, my contracting stomach and the hunger which made my blood run dry through my whole body.

When the headman came up to me in silence and held out a plateful of rice balls and a bowl right in front of my nose, something, probably the shame which clutched my heart, made my trembling arm knock the plate from his hand. But he grabbed me and growled, his upturned lips twitching.

'Don't piss around,' he shouted. 'Hey, don't piss around. Hey, who do you think you are? Someone like you isn't really human. You vermin can only pass on your bad blood. You'll be no good when you're grown up.'

He grabbed me by my shirt front and almost choked me, and he himself was almost panting with rage.

'Listen, someone like you should be throttled while

they're still a kid. We squash vermin while it's small. We're peasants: we nip the bad buds early.'

He was pale and sweating all over his tanned skin and looked like a sick man racked by feverish fits. He sprayed saliva and stinking breath from his rotting gums all over my face, and he was shaking. I thought that I scared him, and rather than giving me pride, that made me quake with a terrible fear.

'Hey, listen,' he shouted. 'We can even throw you off the cliff. No one'll condemn us if we kill you.'

He shook his head of close-cropped white hair and yelled with rage. 'You lot, is any one of you going to tell the constable if I kill him?'

My comrades were hushed with fear as I bent backwards, my neck squeezed, and betrayed me to my face.

'Understand? Hey, do you understand now?'

I closed my eyes and nodded, bitter tears caught in my eyelashes. I understood all too well that I had been abandoned even in my greatest need. The arm choking me loosened, and I pulled myself together after deep breaths and small coughs. I didn't want my comrades who had betrayed me to see the few tears that clung trembling to the dry skin under my eyes.

'Then you eat too,' the headman said.

I refused, my head bowed. He put his arm round my shoulders and stared at me. Then he straightened up, went over to the blacksmith and spoke to him in a low voice. My kit-bag was flung at my knees.

'Stand up,' the headman said.

I stood up, slinging the kit-bag on my shoulder. The blacksmith and other massively well-built men like him, whose sunburned, mudstained skin sagged between their muscles, surrounded me. Dragged by them through the villagers, I came out into the square in front of the school. I was kept there standing and waiting. The villagers gathered before the shed and looked at me. I shivered with cold. It was dark, and the snow had frozen.

After a while the headman came out from the shed. He walked up quickly with long strides. I waited tensely for him.

'Hey,' he said. 'Hey, you.'

My body shook with foreboding.

'We could kill you, but we're going to save you,' he said in one breath and peered at me with eyes that held a dim glow. 'You leave the village tonight, then run a long way away. Remember that if you go to the police, no one'll testify for you. And don't forget that you'll be punished for absconding.'

The headman's statement held various snags and didn't slip smoothly into me. But I nodded, biting my lips. Grabbed by both arms and almost dragged off by the blacksmith and another man, I walked up the road. We walked to the edge of the valley in silence.

To operate the trolley winch, one of the men had to stand astride the mechanism until the trolley started to move. So at first the blacksmith and I squatted down by ourselves in the trolley's small skip with our knees against each other, gloomy inhuman silence enveloping our bodies. Then, as soon as the winch he had swiftly worked started turning, the other man ran noiselessly over the sleepers and got on board. As he sat down he stepped by chance on my bare toes with his snow-covered shoes and made me scream. But the men had become night beasts quaking with anxiety and kept silent, showing no reaction to my groans. Haunted by the rope's snapping sound, I put my dirty fingers in my mouth and noticed the taste of snow, mud and blood on my tongue.

I was about to be banished from the cul-de-sac I had been shut up in. But outside I would also be shut up. I would never be able to escape. Both inside and outside, tough fingers and rough arms were patiently waiting to squash and strangle me.

When the trolley stopped, the blacksmith got out, still grasping his weapon, and I followed him. Then suddenly he attacked me, baring his teeth. I threw myself down and the blacksmith's iron bar whizzed past, grazing the back of my neck, and hit empty space. I got up off the ground and frantically ran up into the dark copse before the iron bar swung back. I went on running into the dark trees, my face beaten by the leaves, my legs entangled by creepers, my skin broken and bleeding all over. Then I fell exhausted into ferns deep in the snow. All I could do was raise myself on my elbows and rub my throat against cold wet-barked shrubs to stifle my sobbing. But the sobs came out incessantly from my mudstained lips and carried in the dark wet air, and that would give away my hiding place to the men who were running wildly around searching for me, calling to each other further down, and to the villagers spurred on by bloodlust. To muffle my sobbing, I panted open-mouthed like a dog. I peered through the dark night air, watching for the villagers' onslaught, and prepared for combat, grabbing lumps of stone in my frozen fists.

But I didn't know what to do to get away through the night forest, fleeing from the brutal villagers, and escape harm. I didn't even know if I still had the strength to run any more. I was only a child, tired, insanely angry, tearful, shivering with cold and hunger. Suddenly a wind blew up, carrying the sound of the villagers' footsteps growing nearer, closing in on me. I got up, clenching my teeth, and dashed into the deeper darkness between the trees and the darker undergrowth.